to one of w
friends sim

with love
Gabriella Internn

Betrayals

Betrayals

The Unpredictability of Human Relations

GABRIELLA TURNATURI

Translated by Lydia G. Cochrane

The University of Chicago Press ❋ *Chicago and London*

GABRIELLA TURNATURI teaches sociology and sociology of culture in the Department of Sciences of Communication at the University of Bologna. She has written many books on emotions, the public sphere, and Georg Simmel. Her works have an interdisciplinary approach, combining methods from sociology and literature studies.

LYDIA G. COCHRANE'S recent translations for the University of Chicago Press include *Wolfgang Amadeus Mozart: A Biography*, by Piero Melograni, and *The Law of God: The Philosophical History of an Idea*, by Rémi Brague.

The University of Chicago Press, Chicago 60637
The University of Chicago Press, Ltd., London
© 2007 by The University of Chicago
All rights reserved. Published 2007
Printed in the United States of America
16 15 14 13 12 11 10 09 08 07   1 2 3 4 5
ISBN-13: 978-0-226-81703-3 (cloth)
ISBN-10: 0-226-81703-2 (cloth)

Originally published as *Tradimenti: L'imprevedibilità nelle relazioni umane.*
© Giangiacomo Feltrinelli Editore Milano, 2000

Library of Congress Cataloging-in-Publication Data

Turnaturi, Gabriella.
  [Tradimenti. English]
  Betrayals : the unpredictability of human relations / by Gabriella Turnaturi ; translated by Lydia G. Cochrane.
    p.   cm.
  Includes bibliographical references (p.   ) and index.
  ISBN-13: 978-0-226-81703-3 (cloth : alk. paper)
  ISBN-10: 0-226-81703-2 (cloth : alk. paper)   1. Betrayal.
  I. Title.
  BJ1500 .B47T8713 2007
  302'.17—dc22

                                                    2006101993

To my son Andrea

Betray. A great word. What is betrayal? They talk of a man betraying his country, his friends, his sweetheart. There must be a moral bond first. All a man can betray is his conscience.

«JOSEPH CONRAD, *Under Western Eyes*»

Contents

Acknowledgments

I wrote this book in 1999 while I was in New York, a city close to my heart. Many things have happened since then. Even though I have continued to follow, with affection and curiosity, the changes that have taken place in American culture and American society, the episodes to which I refer in the text are now past history. My reflections on the nature of betrayal remain the same, however.

During my stay in New York I had the opportunity to exchange ideas with colleagues and friends from New York University and the Remarque Institute. Among such friends I owe particular thanks to Richard Sennett, Allan Silver, and Nadia Urbinati of Columbia University, all of whom gave me highly useful suggestions. Howard Becker not only read the Italian text with great patience but also gave welcome encouragement and help regarding the present edition in English.

My thanks go also to Italian friends with whom I discussed my interpretations of betrayals on many occasions: the psychoanalyst Simona Argentieri, the historian Rosanna De Longis, the sociologists Franco Crespi and Gianfranco Poggi, and Marina Mizzau, a specialist in the psychology of communication. I would also like to thank all of my colleagues and friends in the Dipartimento di Scienze della Comunicazione at the University of Bologna, who dedicated an afternoon to listening to me, and who encouraged me to sharpen certain hypotheses and clarify some assertions. Special thanks to Pier Paolo Giglioli and to his indefatigable critical mind.

As with all of my books, this one owes much to the attention, the rigor, and the love of my husband, who has always been my most severe reader: once more, many thanks.

April 1999

Introduction

What are we talking about when we speak of betrayal? Can we imagine a sociological definition of betrayal that would include all of its various modes, aspects, and forms? To betray whom, what, and—above all—how? Who names and defines the betrayal? Who is betrayed, and who betrays? Does a betrayal necessarily have to be known, hence acknowledged, by both of the subjects for it to be called a betrayal—for it to exist? How does the social definition of betrayal vary, and what is meant by the term in everyday usage? And, finally, how do the moral judgments and social sanctions applied to betrayal vary? These are only some of the questions discernible in the vast and vaguely defined universe of betrayal.

To answer the question of why people betray is nearly impossible. Too much complexity and ambiguity exist in every form of interaction and imbue every relationship; too much complexity and ambiguity inhabit every individual. A number of things—passions and interests, opposing representations of oneself and of others, contradictory but simultaneous needs for membership and separation, and a desire for collectivity and singularity, for protection and emancipation, for trust and for distance—are interwoven in a thousand ways, and they can give rise to infinite types of betrayal. We betray ourselves, our families, our friends, our lovers, our country. We betray out of ambition, for vengeance, through inconstancy, to assert our autonomy, and for a hundred passions and a hundred reasons.

We are used to thinking of betrayal as a self-evident event whose origins we foolishly believe we can reconstruct. Most betrayals, however, seem not to have any obvious cause and no possible rational explanation, either on the part of the betrayer or the betrayed. They resist classification within any known order. If we look at the infinite number of interactions in everyday life, we discover that betrayal is much more common and more widespread that we had supposed, so common, in fact, that we can state that betrayal should be counted among the many possible form of intersubjectivity.

History and literature have always offered infinite examples of betrayal, and the same is true of the cinema, popular songs, and television serials. The dramatic impact of betrayal and the moral judgment passed on it, of course, vary according to the narrative context. In much of contemporary literature, betrayal is no longer presented as a tragic event, and there is an abyss, as Tony Tanner points out, between adultery as narrated by Tolstoy and adultery in our own time as described by John Updike,[1] or between political betrayal in Shakespeare's tragedies and in the novels of John Le Carré. Nonetheless, everyone—intellectuals and ordinary folk, women and men—continues to be fascinated by betrayal narratives.

Hearing or reading a tale of betrayal probably activates a recognition mechanism in us all: Is there anyone who has never betrayed or who has never been betrayed? Betrayal may fascinate us precisely because it is so common; it forms a part of our everyday experience, yet it resists simplistic explanations. Both common and complex, betrayal can never be reduced to one cause, one motive, or one reason. With betrayal, we are faced with the greatest tragedy of human relations: the fact that the other is unknowable.

Judith Shklar lists betrayal among humankind's most widespread, most ordinary vices.[2] Although I disagree with her definition of vice, it is undeniable that betrayal happens frequently and is located within a space and time of happenstance, as relationships form and dissolve. It is also true, however, that the incidence of everyday betrayals (betrayals that occur almost "by chance") rises with increased social complexity and social differentiation, as I shall explain in chapter 5. I say almost "by chance" because what can seem fortuitous to the sociologist can be attributed in other branches of knowledge (psychoanalysis, for example) to motivations and goals, including unconscious ones. Moreover, when sociologists speak of fortuitousness, the term does not imply irrationality, but rather the creativity and the processual character of interaction, which contain and ceaselessly create spaces of loyalty and betrayal.

Even though the forms of betrayal are many, I have chosen to examine them as particular forms of everyday interaction, as common events. Thus I shall treat the terrible ordinary betrayals that strike the heart without warning, that surprise because they come from a friend, a lover, a relative, a colleague. Such betrayals are often inexplicable, turning our life upside down and throwing sudden light on our own frailty and that of others. Great or small, they always involve the definition and redefinition of our own identity; they confront us with a choice about who we want to be, for ourselves and for others.

Every interaction arises and grows around sharing something—even for a short time—with an other: a project to be realized; a relationship to be constructed; a game, an adventure, an ideal, a fleeting pleasure, a secret, a conflict; an affiliation or sense of membership or belonging. In all of these forms of shared experience we act within a common framework; something unites us, if only for a moment, and creates a "We." The birth of a We brings with it the possibility of betrayal, separation, or rupture.

In every form of being and of acting with one another there are obscure zones, secret areas, and margins of ambiguity without which relations and interactions would not survive, but which at the same time mean that betrayal, dramatic or banal, always lies in wait for us. The very fact that our knowledge of the other can never be certain and complete, and that every relationship, if it is to survive, requires discretion and secrecy on both sides, shows that we can never feel sure about what may happen between ourselves and others.

Furthermore, if it is true that not only in every relationship but in every interaction parts of ourselves that we were unaware of come to light, we cannot even be sure that we will never betray. Betrayal, both as an act on our part and as an action we undergo, is always relational and always possible. When we enter into relations with others, a step that is necessary for the construction of our own identity, we put into play our desire to be with the other—but also our desire not to lose ourselves in the other. We want and we need to be with the other, but at the same time, to safeguard our individuality, we want and need to not be so completely with them. This alternation between being fully present in a relationship and not being fully present is where betrayal finds its niche. Role expectations are always tightly interwoven, marking every relationship with ambiguity, ambivalence, and uncertainty. We exist only with and through the other, but if we did not also exist as relatively autonomous individuals we could never encounter the other. It is within this dialectic of being fully present or not that establishing face-to-face contact and setting up a relationship with the other exists, but so, too, does the possibility of betrayal. A completely predictable relationship, transparent in its every moment and aspect, founded on total and reciprocal comprehension, is not only impossible but would congeal the relationship and lead to immobility, hence to the annulment of both subjects. If the encounter with the other necessarily renders me silent, and if identity is constructed through thousands of encounters and interactions, superficial or profound, there can be no transparency, no certain once-and-for-all comprehension between us. We have to run the risk of incomprehension, ambivalence, and misunderstanding; they allow us to be both fully engaged and somewhat withdrawn and to pursue interactions, relations, and encounters without being swallowed up by them.

This is why I have chosen to examine all those betrayals in everyday life that, rather than springing from overwhelming passions or astute machinations, come from being with the other and from the diverse and possible ways in which the encounter occurs—the betrayals that are part of the game of life and cannot be eliminated by any form of intersubjectivity.

In chapter 3 I analyze the relationship between Queen Elizabeth I and the Earl of Essex. Here I am less interested in Essex's strictly political betrayals, his strategic machinations, and his eventual high treason. What I want to investigate is what happens in a relationship marked from the start by ambivalence and expectations of conflict—a relationship that survived (as long as it did survive) precisely thanks to misunderstandings, and that concluded tragically when both parties found their margins of ambiguity reduced, leaving them imprisoned in their roles.

I have devoted chapter 4 to the revelation or concealment of secrets, because it is through secrecy that our being fully present in a relationship or not, our individuality, and intersubjectivity are brought into play in everyday life.

Also in chapter 3 I have attempted to reread the betrayals of Jesus by Judas and Peter in this perspective, as events produced within the formation and dissolution of interactions within everyday life. Thus I focus on betrayal as a sociological event, rather than emphasizing its ethical and moral implications or the ontological perspective of being with the other and being for oneself.

To regard betrayal from the viewpoint of interactions and relations implies concentrating on its processual and interactive character. This perspective does not require a reconstruction of the psychological figure of the betrayed and the betrayer or of their character and psychic traits, a task that some psychologists and psychoanalysts have taken on with notable success.[3] The betrayer and the betrayed become so only through the particular type of interactions and relations that they themselves construct and act out. Neither the betrayer nor the betrayed existed, as such, before those interactions and relations, which implies that, *sociologically*, it is impossible to construct typologies of subjects who have a tendency to be betrayed and other subjects who are betrayers by reason of their psyche.

The system of general values enters into the social definition of betrayal, but so do the rules and the standards that specific subjects set for themselves. The social definition of betrayal changes, not only with respect to general evaluative systems and criteria of judgment, but also with respect to the individual subjects.

Still, even through betrayals are the result of concrete interactions and of the transformation of relations between specific individuals, they take on different forms and a different significance according to historical and social context.

The social relevance, significance, and moral evaluation of betrayals vary according to the symbolic orders and the historical contexts in which the betrayal occurs. This is what I seek to demonstrate in the final chapter.

1

Betrayals

I know thee not, old man; fall to thy prayers.

. . .

Presume not that I am the thing I was,
For God doth know, so shall the world perceive,
That I have turned away my former self;
So will I those that kept me company.

«WILLIAM SHAKESPEARE, *Henry the Fourth, Part II*, 5.5, 47, 56–59»

What Are We Talking about When We Speak of Betrayal?

The meanings of the verb "to betray" are multiple. Leafing through a dictionary we find: to fail to fulfill sacred duties or a moral or juridical obligation to be faithful and loyal; to reveal or divulge something that ought to be kept secret; to delude others by acting in a manner contrary to expectations and to commonly accepted standards of behavior. The original meaning is that of the Latin *trādere*, to deliver or hand over to an enemy, as in the passage from the Gospel according to Luke: "Jesus autem dixit ei: Juda osculo filium hominis tradis" (Jesus said to him, "Judas, would you betray the Son of Man with a kiss?"; Luke 22:48). The first meaning of betrayal thus implies the delivery or transfer of someone (a friend, an ally) or something (a piece of information, a secret) from one side to another.

Betrayal occurs in many forms: there are greater and lesser ones, intolerable ones, and "innocent" ones, and at times one betrayal can contain various others. Adultery, for example, covers several forms of betrayal: failing to respect an obligation and to keep faith, violating intimacy, breaking a pact. Similarly, betraying one's country implies not only breaking an implicit pact of affiliation and an obligation of loyalty; it also includes the betrayal of secrets, of ties of friendship, and of customs. It is a *trādere,* a handing over of information and secrets, but it is above all a "transfer" of the self from one side to the other.

Betrayal is always an act, however: as such, it changes the course and the meaning of relations between persons, breaks ties and pacts, disappoints trust and expectations, and negates membership. Betrayal is by its nature relational, because it presupposes a connection with the other, whether that other is a person, a group, an institution, one's homeland, or the state. Even self-betrayal does not take place in solitude, but results from relations and interactions with others.

All the possible forms of betrayal involve a redefinition of relations in that they produce a double displacement. The person who betrays shifts from one role to another, and as he does so he changes the space he had occupied, forcing out the person betrayed, who changes space and role as well. Betrayal upsets the geography of the positions that subjects assume within a relationship, producing shifts that are not only emotional but that affect identities as well, thus leading to a redrawing of maps. The person who undergoes a betrayal—of any type—cannot avoid the feeling of emptiness that goes along with no longer knowing who and where he or she is. "What am I doing here?" is the question that immediately springs to the mind of those who discover they have been betrayed—precisely because they suddenly find themselves homeless. Betrayal in the now destroys all that previously had been shared. The part of oneself that had been given in trust to the other is violently stripped away.

To speak of betrayal requires previous expectations of loyalty, in both rational and emotive terms, and previously established relations and interactions in which the subjects trusted one another, in part or wholly. There are as many betrayals as there are acts of trust. This is why betrayal always arrives as an unexpected and dramatic event that interrupts ongoing everyday interaction. It is not by chance that in Italian the phrase *a tradimento* can simply mean "suddenly" or "unexpectedly." Even though at times the parties can come to terms again after the shock of a betrayal and the shattering effects it brings with it, their relations will never again be the same. The subjects themselves have changed: both the betrayer and the betrayed are forced to redefine the images that each has of the other and to readjust their respective expectations; they necessarily redefine themselves and their relationship on the basis of that event, which will always remain a watershed moment. Every relationship is formed and thrives by means of the thousand interactions we engage in daily with others, which is why betrayal always throws ordinary life into turmoil.

Betrayal not only *presupposes* shared experience, it also *arises* out of that shared experience—of a secret, of an ideal, of a sense of belonging to something, or of a goal. In that sharing a sort of collective subject is created, the "We," which exists thanks to that joint experience, becomes an entity, and takes on a sacral quality, eventually overwhelming the particular subjects who have brought it into being.

When the We is attacked from the outside, it is reinforced and the sense of sharing is enhanced, but if the We is attacked by one of its component subjects, it displays its full fragility and shatters into a thousand pieces. Abandonment, flight, or simply the obvious desire of one of the subjects to withdraw from the We undermine its existence and its meaning. This is why an internal attack on the We is a true betrayal: it reveals the impermanence and the illusory character of the We. Betrayals occur when the confines of the We are broken in one way or another.[1] Every shared experience runs the risk that one of the subjects will move away from it, because even in the most constraining We the subjects maintain their freedom to come and go and to respect or attack its sacredness.

Betrayal is thus contained within the very idea of sharing; it necessarily implies affiliation or membership:

> "What you are asking me to do is to betray my friends," I said. "I won't do it."
> "You betrayed everything else."
> . . .
> "But what you mean by 'everything,'" I said, "is nothing to me. To be capable of betraying something you must first believe in it."[2]

This exchange occurs in John Banville's novel *The Untouchable*, drawn from the life of Anthony Blunt, the great art historian who worked for both the British intelligence service and the Kremlin. It is the response of the protagonist to a request that he reveal the names of his accomplices and those with whom he shared youthful ideals and projects. Here fiction has a direct replica in reality: Kim Philby, the most famous of Blunt's fellow spies and a man who passed on information to the Soviet Union for a number of years, refused to be labeled a traitor, declaring that, in order to betray, one must first belong. Within himself, Philby had always felt himself to be a Communist and never a part of the community in England.

Whoever abandons a faith, a group, or a community, or who passes from one membership to another is considered a traitor in the name of a previous "life in common." An outsider, a foreigner, or a passerby with no ties of shared experience, no felt membership, can be considered ill-intentioned or cruel and be accused of the most heinous crimes, but he or she cannot be accused of betrayal: "The heretic who abandons a creed is therefore disdained and punished, while the pagan is merely an object of solicitude."[3]

"Betray. A great word. What is betrayal? They talk of a man betraying his country, his friends, his sweetheart. There must be a moral bond first. All a man can betray is his conscience."[4] These are the thoughts of Razumov, the protagonist of Joseph Conrad's *Under Western Eyes*. He expresses them after denouncing

Hadlin, an occasional fellow student who had confided in him, unilaterally deciding to entrust Razumov with his life.

On the basis of this definition of betrayal, Razumov can declare that he never betrayed Hadlin's trust, because there had never been any bond between them.

With anguish and rage, but also with the precision of a sociologist distinguishing between various relational forms, Razumov goes on to ask himself: "By what bond of common faith, of common conviction, am I obliged to let that fanatical idiot drag me down with him? On the contrary—every obligation of true courage is the other way. . . . What can the prejudice of the world reproach me with? Have I provoked his confidence? No! Have I by a single word, look, or gesture given him reason to suppose that I accepted his trust in me? *No!*"[5]

Since faith cannot exist unilaterally—we cannot force someone to trust in us, nor can we decide, independent of the will and the assent of the other, that we wish to trust in him—so also there can be no betrayal where there are not acknowledged, reciprocally accepted relations and interactions of trust. "I trust you even if you don't want me to or don't know it" is a paradoxical statement. In order for there to be betrayal, A not only has to trust in B but B must consciously accept that trust and recognize the tie that unites him to A. We cannot be betrayed by someone that we love but who has always rejected that love, or by someone we unilaterally define as a friend who does not care to be friends with us.

Only the act or series of acts that break a voluntary and conscious relationship of trust can be defined as betrayal. Obviously, one can play on the notion of misunderstanding; one can negate, after the fact, the existence of a relationship of trust in order to shake free of a sense of guilt; and one can ignore the consequences of the betrayal—but such considerations lie beyond an attempted sociological reading of betrayal.

If we adopt Razumov's definition of betrayal, the entire problematic of the ontological responsibility for the other and for the moral ties that bind individuals to one another, independent of the type of relationship they have, is eliminated. Here I am deliberately ignoring the philosophical theme of being with the other and of the fate of necessarily being with the other in order to treat betrayal from the viewpoint of the sociology of everyday relations and interactions.

If the existence of a We is what lays down the conditions for and creates the possibility of betrayal, it is also necessary to consider the types or particular forms of the We that take for granted a sense of affiliation that does not rely on free and conscious membership. I am referring here to being part of a country, a nation, or a community, where loyalty is assumed to be the natural course. Philby or Blunt, for example, could maintain that they never acknowledged their membership in the English community, but no one else doubted that they were a part of the British nation, or that their duties as subjects included loyalty to British institutions. From the point of view of their compatriots, Blunt and Philby were objectively traitors, whereas from their own point of view their withdrawal from the English community permitted them to not consider themselves traitors.

A further question is, In how many ways can the We be betrayed? The many forms of betrayal are strictly correlated with the various types of We that are formed in the making and unmaking of intersubjectivity. For example, where the We must be known only by those who take part in it, as with a sect or a clandestine organization, betrayal consists in revealing the existence of the group. If instead the We exists and is recognized publicly, as in the case of a group of friends, a family, one side in a legal dispute, or a publicly acknowledged couple, betrayal consists in declaring oneself outside of that connection, in disavowing it.

When the We has a public existence but at the same time has a secret life of its own reinforced by symbolic gestures, language, and expressions that exclude nonmembers, betrayal consists in a unilateral decision to throw open the doors to that intimate and private sphere.

In similar fashion, because the We exists by producing and reproducing itself through the attribution of value to certain shared things, experiences, and symbolic manifestations, betrayal of that

We implies unilateral changes in the attribution of value. What was significant and meaningful for both parties loses value and meaning for only one of them.

Finally, when the We becomes an entity independent of the free will of its participating subjects, when it is reified and perceived as something external and immutable, betrayal consists in a sudden withdrawal from that reification on the part of someone who claims the right to change.

The Phenomenology of Betrayal

Betrayal is a process situated in a shared space and time, constructed with others, whether the other is one individual or a group—of friends, a family, a community, or a nation. This perspective enables us to isolate some specific and constant aspects of betrayal.

BETRAYING A RELATIONSHIP

Betrayal always involves the abandonment of a relationship or a group, but rather than an aggressive act directed toward the other or others, it is a direct, more or less intentional act aimed at destroying that relationship or withdrawing from it.

Georg Simmel states that faithfulness, from the sociological standpoint, is "one of those very general modes of conduct that become important in all interactions among men, no matter how different they may be materially or sociologically." He states further that faithfulness or loyalty "is the emotional reflection of the autonomous life of the relation, unperturbed by the possible disappearance of the motives which originally engendered the relation."[6] Hence being faithful is not focused on the other's well-being, nor on loyalty, but on maintaining the relationship.

If faithfulness is oriented to the maintenance of the relationship rather than to the possession of the other, in symmetrical fashion betrayal is not focused on the abandonment of the other, but rather on the abandonment of the relationship. One does not betray the individual subject, but the specific relationship.

The betrayal of a pact of reciprocal loyalty and trust, both in friendship and in love, is never simply an aggressive gesture toward the other, but rather a sort of symbolic declaration of estrangement, a way of setting oneself at a distance from the relationship. Although betrayal is not always the result of a determined and conscious decision or of an intention to destroy the relationship, it always involves a redefinition of that relationship and it changes the roles of the subjects involved. As a betrayal takes place, it reveals not only to the betrayed but also to the betrayer that a change or redefinition is taking place. In this sense it becomes a sort of revelation or epiphany.

The protagonist in Paul Auster's novel *Leviathan* gives in to an impulse to read his wife's secret diary in a moment of conjugal crisis, something that he had never before dared to do. With this act he betrays her trust in him, and in doing so the vague sense of unease that he had felt before changes into a desire to flee, to remove himself from a relationship that no longer is satisfactory: "Standing there at that moment . . . I found myself gripped by a tremendous urge to read those pages. In retrospect, I understand that this meant our life together was already finished, that my willingness to break this trust proved that I had given up any hope for our marriage, but I wasn't aware of it then."[7]

COLLABORATION IN BETRAYAL

Precisely because betrayal is relational, the subjects—that is, the betrayed and the betrayer—almost always collaborate, consciously or unconsciously, to produce it. In order for A to betray B, B has to have trusted A, and they both have to have constructed some form of shared experience, established tacit rules, and nourished common expectations. B also collaborates in the betrayal by trusting A totally, thus making manipulation or seduction possible.

Judith Shklar claims that psychological collaboration is a subtle and by no means rare variant of betrayal pure and simple.[8] We can induce others to betray us by being passive or else by enabling the other to play the role of betrayer for us and with us.

Let us return to Peter, the protagonist of *Leviathan*, as he reads his wife's diary. He states: "By the time I reached the last paragraph, her conclusion was already self-evident, a thing that no longer needed to be expressed. 'I have never loved Peter,' she wrote. 'It was a mistake to think I ever could. Our life together is a fraud.'" Only by reading these words does Peter realize that he has been skillfully led to betray his wife's trust in him, that their marriage is already finished, and that Delia wants him to play the betrayer. As Auster tells it, Peter continues: "The pages were open on the desk, and Delia had just asked me to go into the room for her. She must have understood that I would notice them. Assuming that was true, it was almost as if she were inviting me to read what she had written. In all events, that was the excuse I gave myself that night, and even now I'm not so sure I was wrong. It would have been just like her to act indirectly, to provoke a crisis she would never have to claim responsibility for."[9]

Even when we deny its existence, we actively collaborate in betrayal; consciously or unconsciously unaware of it, we deceive ourselves in one way or another. In relations of love or friendship we often choose to ignore every signal, every evidence of betrayal, even when the other scatters them along the path just so they will be discovered. In such cases, not only do both parties lend support to the betrayal; it becomes a form of the relation itself, kept alive precisely thanks to a deliberate eyes-closed policy, to self-deception, and to the fact that within the relationship a clear division of roles has been set up between the betrayer and the betrayed.

Surviving relationships can also depend on a reciprocal game of ambivalence in which the two subjects continually exchange roles as betrayed and betrayer. Henry Green's novel *Doting* presents a happily married middle-aged couple who, although they do not arrive at the point of adultery, have a marriage in which small reciprocal betrayals, flirting, and amorous flings play an important part.[10] The two partners betray one another, and each of them plays the part of the betrayer and the betrayed, acting out scenes of unfulfilled passion and restlessness that find no other way to express themselves. The relationship between these two profoundly disturbed and ambivalent people is a satisfactory one precisely because of their reliance on mutual betrayal and their constant shift between being present in the relationship and being withdrawn from it.

BETRAYAL AND COMMUNICATION

Betrayal lurks in every form of communication, and every communication contains the risk of betrayal. I am not referring to a deliberate use of fallacious words and statements intended to deceive but rather to the perception of what has just been said. A hears things that B has not said; B believes that he or she has said one thing but has in fact communicated another. There is an ambiguity in communication, thanks not only to the polysemia of language and the proliferation of the signified but also because possible interpretations are infinite in number, changing not only according to the subjects involved but thanks also to the type of interaction they establish.

Not ever completely knowing the other, as he presents himself to us, nor how we seem in his eyes—the fact of "not knowing the relationship," as Franco La Cecla suggests—brings disturbance, interference, and incorrect inferences to every act of communication and gives rise to misunderstandings.[11] Such misunderstandings are not so much due to defective communication as they are to what Vladimir Jankélévitch calls an unawareness of relations, an unavoidable vagueness that accompanies individuals as they enter into relationships with one another.[12] Within this knowing and not knowing, words lose their clear contours as well, and the meaning that words convey to one person and to the other is hard to gauge. This lack of full awareness of the other and of oneself invites not only misunderstanding but also the possibility of a betrayal, interpreted as a failure to live up to the expectations and the trust invested in the communication. I believe that the other understands the sense in which I use a particular word, and the other believes the same of his words, and we initiate interactions and establish relations on the basis of those suppositions. We tend to attribute the most obvious meaning to a word, following the dictates of ordinary language and the context in which it is used, but the contexts in which we communicate contain uncertain definitions and have shifting confines, which lends uncertainty to both the communication and the relationship itself. Both parties attempt to place the meaning of words within a context they think pertains and in which they feel at home. Misunderstandings, mistakes, and unilateral definitions accumulate, to the point that they provide the structure for relations that continue to be built up, even when the parties to them never wholly comprehend one another.

One or both of the parties in the relationship may suddenly realize that they are not understanding each other, that they have misinterpreted or have been misinterpreted, in a revelation that is experienced as a deliberate betrayal, as a rupture of reciprocal understanding. In an instant, the other appears in all of his or her alterity, as an unknown quantity or someone totally unfamiliar. This cognitive gap, which in turn rests on a communication gap, gives rise to a perception of betrayal as an abandonment, as an end to the mutual misunderstanding that was the lifeblood of the relationship.

"I thought I understood"; "I thought I had made you understand"; "What I meant to say"; "What I thought that you meant to say"—these are all things that we exclaim, panic stricken, when the misunderstanding is unveiled, and when a misunderstanding is perceived late in the game, it seems a betrayal. Paradoxically, it is often when the parties reach a clarification that they feel themselves betrayed—that is, when one of them no longer plays the misunderstanding game and things and words become intolerably clear and unambiguous.

PERCEPTIONS OF BETRAYAL

For there to be betrayal, the act must be so perceived and so defined by either the person betrayed or the betrayer. Only they can name it as a betrayal, acknowledge it, and call it into being.

No one can force someone else to "feel betrayed" against his or her will, but it is quite possible to manipulate someone into feeling betrayed, even in the absence of a genuine betrayal, as is the case with Iago and Othello. Iago states, "I'll pour this pestilence into his ear" (*Othello*, 2.3.350; Bevington, 1142). Thus, when Iago and Othello see Cassio plead with Desdemona to intercede for him with her husband, Iago pours his "poison" of suspicion into Othello's mind, even though Cassio does nothing improper:

OTHELLO: Was not that Cassio parted from my wife?
IAGO: Cassio, my lord? No, sure, I cannot think it,
   That he would steal away so guilty-like,
   Seeing you coming.

«*Othello*, 3.3.37–40; Bevington, 1143»

Only a few allusive words, and the perception of betrayal is constructed. From that moment on, Othello feels himself betrayed, and no one can persuade him otherwise. Little or nothing has gone into constructing that perception, but demolishing it proves to be impossible.

The proofs of a supposed betrayal—be they genuine or false—take on the look of truth precisely because every gesture and every word is interpreted through the perception of being betrayed. Moreover, while it is impossible to prove faithfulness or loyalty, it is always possible to find or to construct proofs of infidelity and betrayal. Belief is a conviction that is based less on proof than on the absence of contradictory proof.[13] Whereas Iago can construct a nonexistent betrayal on Desdemona's part, thus unleashing jealousy, that "green-ey'd monster," in the mind and the heart of Othello, Desdemona can do nothing to prove her fidelity.

Nor can Cordelia do anything to prove her affection for King Lear, her father:

... Unhappy that I am, I cannot heave
My heart into my mouth. I love your Majesty
According to my bond; no more nor less.

«*King Lear*, 1.1.91–93; Bevington, 1174»

To prove faithfulness, loyalty, filial love, or friendly affection would require confirmation of everyday reality; it would involve proving something that normally has no need of proof. For that reason, there are no instruments, no ways to prove it. "I love your Majesty according to my bond, no more nor less" is not a provable assertion or a demonstrable fact; it is just a fact. Its contrary, lack of love or filial betrayal, can be perceived, however. If in no other way, it can be demonstrated because something contrary to expectations has taken place. Anything—the use of a particular expression, a tone of voice, a glance—can be interpreted as a signal of abandonment and a confirmation of a supposed betrayal. This is what happens to Lear. Cordelia's words are not what he wanted to hear:

> How, how, Cordelia! Mend your speech a little,
> Lest you may mar your fortunes.

« *King Lear*, 1.1.94–95; Bevington, 1174 »

This is as if to say, "Tell me what I expected to hear." When this does not happen, Lear repudiates Cordelia, the most beloved and the most devoted of his daughters, as a betrayer.

To perceive an action, a gesture, or a statement as a betrayal induces the hearer to reinterpret, hence to recast, the entire past of the relationship in the light of betrayal. All events are seen, in retrospect, as confirmation of the betrayal, as preparation for and a warning of a deception. What has occurred, although it is part of a history and a relationship, becomes attributed to the perfidy and the ill will of the betrayer and to the ingenuousness of the betrayed. Hence it is seen as the act of just one person.

Can we speak of betrayal if the person betrayed is never aware of it? Certainly not, if betrayal is based uniquely in awareness, as Shakespeare states, through Othello:

> He that is robb'd, not wanting what is stol'n,
> Let him not know't, and he's not robbed at all.

« *Othello*, 3.3.347–48; Bevington, 1147 »

If we regard betrayal as a form of relationship, we cannot deny that, even if only one of the subjects is aware of it, the betrayal nevertheless changes both the relationship and the individuals. The betrayal is there, it encumbers the relationship even if it is perceived and experienced as such only by the person who violates an implicit or explicit pact—that is, by the person who shatters a relationship of trust—although the betrayed party (an individual or a group) is still unaware of the betrayal or does not yet perceive it as such. The one doing the betraying either attempts to distract attention by assuming an attitude of greater secrecy or defensiveness or else tries to hide a sense of guilt behind an aggressive stance. The betrayer's behavior toward the other changes, which creates a change in the betrayed as well and modifies the relationship. All it takes to introduce a change in the relationship, in fact, is for one of the parties to that relationship to name and acknowledge the betrayal, even if only internally. Conversely, one can feel betrayed even if the other or the others do not perceive themselves as betrayers. The betrayer can feel trapped, consciously or unconsciously, by contradictions inherent in the human mind, deceiving himself and imagining himself to be loyal.[14] In this case, betrayal is perceived only by the betrayed, but it will nonetheless leave its mark on the interaction. Once the other is perceived as a betrayer, even without explicit accusations, proofs, or admissions, the relationship necessarily changes.

CHANGE

In every form of interaction, every lasting relationship, one of the subjects can change, slowly or suddenly modifying his ways of thinking about himself, of narrating his views, and of relating not only to the other but to the world at large. Anyone who is undergoing phases of change tends to eliminate routines and habits that, over the course of time, had become rules of behavior and tacit pacts: he or she abandons a universe of shared meaning. The very fact of the change appears to the other as a betrayal, because it erodes all reliance on what had been certain, all mutual understanding within the universe of the habitual.

The person who changes becomes unpredictable, even unrecognizable, for the other. Change, moving away from routine, is perceived as a form of abandonment, as if the changed person had chosen a route leading outside the We, leaving the We by the wayside. This change is experienced as a betrayal, not only within a pair connected by love or friendship but also by a group or community that finds it difficult to accept the fact that one of its members might adopt new parameters of judgment. Every change is perceived as a threat to the status quo and brings with it the suspicion of a possible betrayal. Every betrayal is an unexpected break that subverts implicit or explicit rules.

"I don't recognize you any more" is the accusation most often thrown at the presumed betrayer, irrespective of his intentions and concrete acts. Any change comes to be equated with betrayal, even though we all change something of ourselves in the ongoing process of everyday life and the construction of our own identity and our relations with others, just as we tend to conserve certain other things. Simmel writes in this regard: "Perhaps the greatest tragedy of human conditions springs from (among other things) the utterly unrationalizable and constantly shifting mixture of the stable and variable elements of our nature."[15]

The individual continually moves in new directions, in an incessant exploration of the self and the world. This is why he or she can occasionally drift away not only from relations that seemed destined to last forever but also from parts of the self that are no longer considered meaningful or that are changing. Simmel continues: "In doing so, they [new interests, aims, capacities] turn us away from earlier conditions with a sort of unfaithfulness, which is neither quite innocent, since there exist some bonds which must now be broken, nor quite guilty, since we are no longer the persons we were when we entered the relationship; the subject to whom the unfaithfulness could be imputed has disappeared."[16]

Often the shift within an individual from one self to another is perceived as betrayal. In such cases, the betrayer's fault is to have become different and to be moving forward alone rather than in synchrony with the other. Only when change in the other is accepted and welcomed as a challenge to redefine oneself and redefine the relationship is change not perceived as a betrayal. But for that to be possible, the one who has changed or is changing must not hide the fact, but rather involve the other or others in it.

BETRAYAL IS ASYMMETRICAL

Betrayal is the locus of asymmetry: between our expectations and reality; between the image we have of the other and the other; between our sensibility and the knowledge that the other has of us; between our reading of gestures and words and what those gestures and words were intended to communicate; between the rules implicit in a certain interaction and the breaking of those rules; between moving along and staying put; between the one who changes and the one who refuses to change; between attention and inattention.

Which one has moved outside the relationship? Which one has changed, or which one has stopped following the other's development and is no longer really paying attention? And when that happens, is the betrayal not perhaps reciprocal, in the sense of a mutual abandonment of the relationship?

Reciprocity is annulled by an asymmetry in the two parties' perception of the betrayal, and also by an asymmetry between the fast pace of change on one side and a slowness to focus on that change on the other.

BETRAYAL IS ASYNCHRONIC

In betrayals the timing is never well synchronized. For the person who is aware of betraying, time can seem extremely long, and often he or she deliberately accelerates matters, intentionally scattering traces so that they will be discovered, putting an end to what had seemed an endless process. For the person who discovers that he or she is being betrayed, on the other hand, everything happens in an instant. The opposite can also be true, however: the betrayer can perceive the time between the betrayal and its discovery (or its confession) as swift, because everything has crystallized in the moment of revelation, while that same time can be felt as very long by the betrayed, who in that same instant glimpses an entire past, a history that he or she had failed to grasp.

"Why didn't you tell me right away?" "How could you have hidden a secret for so long?" "Why are you telling me this only now?" The betrayed almost always says (or thinks) these things. They express the hurt inflicted not only by the betrayal itself but by an awareness of time expropriated—time removed from common experience, time of which the betrayed was unaware. Suddenly that past time spent together seems sown with hidden acts and hidden meaning; it becomes a time of deceit and solitude.

The one who betrays has a different perception of time and tends to isolate the betrayal, setting it apart as an interruption— the rupture of a continuity that can always be picked up again. The betrayer often asks, and in good faith, "What does one betrayal mean in comparison with a lifetime together founded on loyalty and fidelity?" For him or her, the time of the betrayal is not part of shared time, but rather belongs to a parallel time that cannot be measured.

In Harold Pinter's *Betrayal*, a play in which all the characters betray one another, the only thing that seems to count morally and emotionally for the various characters is how long the reciprocal betrayals have been kept secret and how long they have gone on. The hurt seems to be inflicted not by a betrayal of ties of love or friendship but rather by a protracted time period filled with secret gestures, furtive acts, and unsaid words. The time thought to have been centered on a We and to have been imbued with shared meaning and common acts suddenly appears meaningless and not subject to measurement, filled with unknown acts that occurred at undetermined moments. The person betrayed can no longer reconstruct the time that had been spent together, because there were moments that he or she did not participate in or experience. The temporal sequence of those acts no longer coincides with the betrayer's time. In betrayal, time appears to be at once too long and too short. For the one who has been betrayed, the other has lived a double time of infinite reverberations—one a time of presence and the other a time of absence. This, I believe, is what is meant by the expression "to live a double life": it refers to this double time, one time of being fully present or not, of being here but also being elsewhere.

The one who betrays, with a magician's sleight of hand, makes all the time supposedly lived together suddenly disappear, and the betrayed is left cheated of that shared time. This explains the sense of being lost: not only "I don't know what I'm doing here any more" but also "I don't even know where I was then."

Finally, the passage of time can mitigate the effects of the betrayal and its importance for both the betrayer and the betrayed. Any individual defines and evaluates betrayal differently according to the context in which it arrives and the life phase he or she is going through. Something held to be an unpardonable betrayal can come to seem merely a stupid deceit or a necessary rite of passage. What had seemed unjustifiable can be revisited with greater tolerance. Betrayals that in one phase of our lives would have seemed to us unworthy and execrable can seem almost innocent in another phase.

The passage from adolescence to adulthood, for example, often brings with it a different attitude toward and evaluation of betrayal. Adolescents cannot think of themselves, either in the present or in their future adult life, as betrayed or betrayers, because identity is constructed through relations with others, hence through trust. Adolescents unfailingly condemn betrayal, which seems to them not only a threat to a fundamental ethical order in which actions and judgments are inscribed but also a serious threat of abandonment. In adolescence we demand an absolute loyalty and total faithfulness. Precisely because the adolescent identity is still fragile and feeling oneself part of a We is fundamental to self-affirmation, adolescents are emotionally more exposed to feeling themselves betrayed. Every promise unfulfilled, every secret disclosed, is experienced as an enduring wound, and when adults who have been trusted or unconditionally admired fail to live up to ideal expectations, the adolescent feels profoundly betrayed and abandoned. With greater maturity these betrayals will be evaluated differently, and unless they become fixed in the young person's awareness as traumatic events, they will be seen as necessary to growth and the formation of personal autonomy. Primal trust—the trust established in the first months of life—can be undermined by an excess of frustration, but also by an excess of gratification that leaves no room for the child to learn to trust himself or herself. The child who is never disappointed or frustrated will not learn to tolerate waiting, a quality necessary in every trust-based relationship.

James Hillman claims that early trust must be shattered if relations are to evolve, and that a crisis, a rupture characterized by betrayal, is necessary if the individual is to learn to distinguish between the self and the other, hence to both trust and mistrust. Learning to trust and learning that we can be betrayed are part of the formation of the individual human being.[17]

The experience of betrayal thus enters into the socialization process as a necessary part of growing up; it aids loss of innocence and leads to understanding that we are all exposed not only to the risk of being betrayed but also to the possibility of becoming betrayers.

Betrayals—great and small, committed or undergone—appear as betrayals only years later, and only in a phase of identity redefinition. Acts that had seemed insignificant come to be reinterpreted in the light of sufferings undergone or inflicted on others and through a richer store of experience. In self-narration they suddenly appear as betrayals.

Betrayers and betrayed thus become so, not only in respect to the other but also in respect to the various narratives of the self that everyone constructs in different phases of life.

The Emotions of Betrayal

Much of what has been written and theorized regarding betrayal restricts the capacity and the will to betray to a few figures, always portrayed as cruel, ill-intentioned, and avid, and in all cases and in any event destined by the narrative to perish, be defeated, or be punished for their betrayals.

In literature and in history from Judas to our own day, there are no positive figures of traitors or betrayers (except for Flavius Josephus, who is credited with using betrayal for good ends), and no instances of betrayals that are not attributable to evil or to some sort of perversion.[18] Shakespeare, for example, portrays Richard III not only as ill-intentioned and cruel but also as monstrous and deformed, a person not to be trusted and marked by nature with the sign of the betrayer.

Richard himself tells us that his horrible nature and horrible aspect make him necessarily traitorous:

> I, that am rudely stamp'd, and want love's majesty
> To strut before a wanton ambling nymph;
> I, that am curtail'd of this fair proportion,
> Cheated of feature by dissembling nature,
> Deform'd, unfinish'd, sent before my time
> Into this breathing world, scarce half made up,
> And that so lamely and unfashionable
> That dogs bark at me as I halt by them—
> Why I, in this weak piping time of peace,
> Have no delight to pass away the time,
> Unless to see my shadow in the sun
> And descant on mine own deformity.
> And therefore, since I cannot prove a lover
> To entertain these fair well-spoken days,
> I am determined to prove a villain
> And hate the idle pleasures of these days,
> Plots have I laid, inductions dangerous,
> By drunken prophecies, libels, and dreams.

«*Richard the Third*, 1.1.13–33; Bevington, 672»

Even psychoanalysis tends to treat betrayal as a pathology, supporting a widespread notion that some personalities are more inclined to treachery than others.[19] Betrayal is presented as deriving from events in a person's past history or from defective socialization; it is symptomatic of a disturbed personality. Moreover, as a symptom of disturbance, it can be treated, mitigated, and avoided. It is paradoxical that psychoanalysis, which arose as a science of ambivalence and the unspoken and which, a century ago, shattered the myth of a transparent self-awareness, should take refuge in pathology where betrayal is concerned. Although it is true that betrayal can take on pathological forms and be manifested in some individuals as a compulsion, as something they cannot help doing repeatedly, to consider it uniquely as a psychological disturbance makes the thousand small everyday betrayals in which we are all now the betrayed and now the betrayer completely incomprehensible. Moreover, to treat betrayal as a symptom in a disturbed or suffering personality reduces it to the act itself, to one person's choice, and removes it from the relational dimension. It denies betrayal as a product, conscious or unconscious, of relations, relationships, and interactions.

Even as fine a scholar of institutions and interactions as Shklar attempts to exorcize betrayal by calling it an "ordinary vice." Although Shklar recognizes that betrayal is one of the commonest acts in everyday life, she sees the exercise of certain virtues as capable of warding it off or exorcizing it.[20]

In their study "The Mask of Integrity," Robert and Joyce Hogan show how traitors and impostors are almost always "people with admirable characteristics: intelligence, social poise, self-confidence, charisma, and charm."[21] Although the Hogans do not adopt the idea that traitors are necessarily deviants, they nonetheless attempt to define the capacity and the desire to betray and limit these to a few specific personality types.

In my opinion, using psychoanalysis, psychology, or sociology to trace constants typical of the figure of the betrayer or the traitor still reflects a need to think of betrayal as something that can be circumscribed and predicted, hence to think of a propensity to betray as something that can be diagnosed, subjected to treatment, or avoided. The social sciences—much like the literary narratives—end up exorcizing betrayal by describing and delineating the figure and the personality of betrayers.

If the figure of the betrayer can be constructed, so can its mirror image, that of the betrayed. The person betrayed is described and classified as having a weak personality and as ingenuous, excessively trusting, or overly generous. Even this description is oriented toward exorcizing fear of betrayal because it leads us to think that all we need is wisdom, acuity, intelligence, and a proper balance between trust and distrust to avoid being betrayed.

The concept of betrayal as the product of individual will is in fact much more tranquilizing than its contrary—that is, that betrayal arises out of interaction, out of the formation of relations in which the individuals involved do not always succeed in maintaining conscious and coherent control. To suppose that predetermined figures of the betrayed and the betrayer exist, and that everyone can avoid betrayal through the exercise of will or by submitting to psychotherapy, is obviously more reassuring than the thought that we can all become betrayers or be betrayed, according to our interactions and to the parts of ourselves that those interactions bring to light.

But if betrayal is just as much an integral part of social life as loyalty is, why is it so feared? Why does it always bring such suffering?

Probably it is the relational nature of betrayal that makes it so feared. Always and in all circumstances betrayal involves the rupture of a pact, the negation of the principle of cohesion, and a threat to the possibility of *all* relations. Whether one betrays another individual or a community of which one is a part, the act implies breaking some form of social bond. Above all and on the symbolic level, it negates the principle of cohesion on which ties, bonds, and loyalties rest. Precisely because it threatens the survival of the relationship itself or of the group, betrayal is the threat to the social order most to be feared; it is the most significative symbolic break. To be betrayed by someone awakens the fear of also being betrayed by others, if not by everyone. When a We is shattered, we fear that every other We of which we are a part might collapse. Uncertainty takes the place of all previous security, and everything seems fragile, precarious, and illusory. In this sense, betrayal is a traumatic experience that destabilizes identity, because it throws into crisis both interpersonal trust and trust in oneself. Among all intersubjective experiences, betrayal is certainly the one most loaded with emotions. Only love, which often accompanies it, has the same complexity and emotional force.

Betrayals, from the most trivial to the gravest, inevitably bring in their train a web of emotions that affect the betrayer and the betrayed in equal measure. Betrayal, and the narratives of betrayal that have been and remain so popular, owe their emotional impact to their perverse fascination.

Betrayal always catches all parties to it unaware, even when it is deliberate and their intersubjectivity is fraught with alternating frustrations and gratifications, confirmations of loyalty and disavowals. Above all, betrayal finds us vulnerable; it bares our fragility and our dependence, even within our proclaimed autonomy. We suddenly find ourselves at the mercy of others, deceived, mocked, defrauded of portions of our identity and our life. The other or the others have, above all, robbed us of trust; they have stranded us right in the middle of what had been a shared experience. Once we have been betrayed by friends, lovers, a spouse, parents, or children, we can no longer pronounce the word "We." The We has been annihilated; it no longer exists and it makes no sense to refer to it. The "I" betrayed and the "You" betrayer remain irremediably dissociated and separate. Confusion, a sense of lost moorings, and solitude accompany the immediate awareness of abandonment: to be betrayed in fact means, above all, to be abandoned.

We are forced to erase the image of ourselves that we have constructed together with the other, the image of the other that we have created, and the image of ourselves as part of a shared experience. In this sense, betrayal is a devastating experience because it forces us to redefine ourselves, to raise questions about the other and about ourselves in combination with the other. Who are we, now that we are alone and abandoned? How do we begin to tell our story, and where do we begin? Why have we been betrayed—abandoned? What have we done to deserve this death blow?

For all the negative emotions that the annulment of the other can trigger—anger, rage, scorn, hatred, resentment—betrayal always and inevitably also sets off negative emotions turned inward, toward oneself. To be betrayed denotes an immediate loss of self-esteem: we feel ourselves diminished, scorned, and even guilty of having in some fashion done something to merit betrayal. We can slip into self-pity and depression; we soon develop an image of ourselves as a victim, incapable of discerning or understanding what goes on around us, as well as an image of the other as unfaithful and wicked.

In accounts of women's reactions to betrayal in love one woman is quoted as declaring, "I felt like a fool. I mean, if you're half smart you're supposed to know something is wrong." Another states, "I wanted him dead; at least there is some dignity in being a widow." A third adds that she feels as if her life had been declared worthless. Everything that she had had, everything she had believed in, suddenly meant nothing. Wandering around her house the previous night she looked over fifteen years of memories and shared history: pictures, photos, furniture that suddenly seem to her rubbish waiting for a garage sale.[22] The way these betrayed women tell their stories highlights how resentment toward the other is accompanied by a loss of self-esteem or sense of annihilation.

By almost nonchalantly interrupting the routine of daily life and the tranquil flow of emotions, betrayal unhinges the self-image because it breaks off its narrative. Being betrayed is an experience that cannot be located within a temporal continuity: to the contrary, it is an interruption. Life comes to be related in the light of that shattered continuity; there is a *before* the betrayal and an *after* it. This experience of a life interrupted is necessarily accompanied by a perception of a shattered self that can tell its tale only in terms of the wound received and the break—that is, in terms of before and after. Long after the event, anyone who has been involved in a betrayal, either as betrayer or betrayed, tells about it on the basis of that experience, seen as supremely significant and fundamental to the self: "A paradox of betrayal is the *fidelity* which both betrayed and betrayer keep, after the event, to its bitterness."[23]

This creates negative emotions turned alternately toward the other and toward ourselves; we oscillate between a desire for revenge and accepting our own guilt. The anger and the rage unleashed by betrayal are emotions that help somehow to reestablish self-respect and preserve dignity, because a person betrayed redefines himself or herself as someone who does not simply undergo interaction, but rather controls it by passing from the role of victim to that of protagonist.

The betrayed must work hard to pick up the thread of the narrative again and overcome the trauma of the interruption. This is only possible through an acknowledgment and acceptance of the betrayed self, not through denial. Reacting to betrayal by betraying, thus in turn denying all that had happened before, or by refusing to recognize either oneself or the other, leads to an even more profound devastation of one's own identity, because it involves self-betrayal.

The Fascination of Betrayal

When someone speaks of the emotions connected with betrayal, we immediately think of the person who has been betrayed, almost as if the betrayer felt no emotions. Why is this so? The commonly shared image of the betrayer as ill-intentioned and cruel, as someone who acts only on the basis of personal interests, excludes the possibility that somebody might also betray simply because the very idea of betrayal elicits excitement and emotions. Certainly, it is easier to accept a betrayal if we think that it is motivated by interest; it is not universally accepted that some can betray for the sheer pleasure of it. Still, passions and interests, reasons and emotions are often thickly intertwined in the heart of the betrayer, and it is hard to say with certainty exactly what urged him or her to act. From a moral point of view a betrayal committed for the pleasure of betrayal seems even more reprehensible than one committed for personal interest, but even though we may prefer to ignore it, it is nonetheless a case that deserves analysis within a phenomenology of betrayal.

The vast literature that portrays the world of spies, secret agents, and double agents or that refers to seducer-betrayers often stresses the attraction of betrayal. In the broad gamut of betrayals that appear in almost all of Shakespeare's works he gives a glimpse of the role that the temptation of betrayal plays, along with that of ambition and a thirst for power.

One prime example of this is the story of King Richard III who, when he was duke of Gloucester, betrays everyone and everything in order to become king of England, and who is so embroiled in a tightening whirl of betrayals that he continues to deceive others even when it is no longer necessary, to the point of deriving pleasure from inducing others to betray. What urges him on is not only ambition and a thirst for power but a passion for overturning all order, every loyalty. After killing Edward of Lancaster, Prince of Wales, with his own hands, there seem to be no other obstacle to his achieving his goals, and yet something irresistibly draws him to Lady Anne, Edward's widow, whom he induces to betray the memory of her beloved spouse in the very moment of her greatest grief, as she is shedding hot tears over the body of her husband's father, King Henry VI. Gloucester takes pleasure not only in seducing his enemy's widow but in turning her into a creature like himself, in making her a betrayer. With clever words and subtly seductive arguments, Gloucester shortly persuades Lady Anne not only to forgive him but to submit to him. Thus all order is overturned; there is no longer any separation between evil and good, and in the instant when the princess betrays the memory of her husband, all betrayal is legitimate. Everything is permitted, and the future king is triumphant because he has made betrayal an obvious, necessary, and almost natural behavior. Not only does he work for evil, betraying friends and relatives, but—as Lady Anne's reaction confirms—betrayal is part of the nature of things. For Gloucester, this does not make his image more negative, but reinforces it. If he can lead even those who have every reason to hate him to bow to his fascination, if with his betrayals he can prompt other betrayals, his power is unlimited:

> What! I that kill'd her husband and his father,
> To take her in her heart's extremest hate,
> With curses in her mouth, tears in her eyes,
> The bleeding witness of my hatred by,
> Having God, her conscience, and these bars against me,
> And I no friends to back my suit withal
> But the plain devil and dissembling looks?
> And yet to win her! All the world to nothing!
> Ha!

«*Richard the Third*, 1.2.23–41; Bevington, 637»

In the future King Richard it is the pleasure of betrayal as the subversion of all order and the joy he takes in transforming the world into a universe of betrayals that force him into a compulsion that, like all obsessions, makes him unable to refrain from betrayal.

In the case of spies and secret agents, on the other hand, the emotions connected with betrayal are multiple and the fascination with betrayal is more complex. Many biographies and autobiographies of spies relate a complex mix of emotions and pleasures that have as much to do with the body as they do with the intellect. Anyone whose profession it is to betray, to act as a secret agent or a double agent, must be ever vigilant, always self-aware, always ready not only to betray but to capture every tiny movement, every gesture of the opponent. Part of the pleasure lies in this obligatory and ceaseless vigilance and in feeling one's own mind become sharper, more subtle, and ready for anything. It is the pleasure of feeling oneself totally unified, totally in command of one's own senses and mind. There is a thrill in risking all and in risking discovery for the slightest oversight. Once that emotion and that sensation of total command of the self have been experienced it is hard to turn back. Spies continue to do their jobs not only because they have to (it is not easy to resign from spying), and not for money or for ideological motives, but because they find the giddy sensation that accompanies it inexorably attractive.

But there is another vertigo that seizes the professional betrayer when he looks over the edge of an abyss at his own swirling self-images. The secret agent is aware of his duplicity: he knows he is playing more than one role and that his "I" is multiple, and he knows that he should say to himself: "I am not what I seem to be; I can doubt the world around me and perhaps should even do so." For the betrayer—for all betrayers, and not just spies—the world that surrounds us loses its obviousness and appears as simply one of many possible versions of reality and truth. In a certain sense, the person who betrays and is aware of his own duality—of the disconnect between what is and what appears to be—enjoys the epistemological privilege of glimpsing possible worlds and probing behind and beyond appearances. He becomes aware of realities more complex than apparent reality, which is in itself complex and multiple. This epiphany of the possible can make the game of betrayal positively voluptuous. Here I am using the term "game" quite consciously, because once the pleasure principle becomes dominant, betrayal becomes an end in itself—precisely as with some games of chance—and is detached from all possible judgment.

"We were latter-day Gnostics, keepers of a secret knowledge, for whom the world of appearances was only a gross manifestation of an infinitely subtler, more real reality known only to the chosen few. . . . Thus, for us, *everything* was *itself and at the same time something else.*" This is how the protagonist of John Banville's *The Untouchable* describes the pleasure of betrayal. He conveys the fascination of a reality that is never the same and of a continual, ever-present uncertainty that stimulates and excites rather than terrifying. The same character later states:

> In the spy's world, as in dreams, the terrain is always uncertain. You put your foot on what looks like solid ground and it gives way under you and you go into a kind of free fall, turning tail over tip and

clutching on to things that themselves are falling. This instability, this myriadness that the world takes on, is both the attraction and the terror of being a spy. Attraction, because in the midst of such uncertainty you are never required to *be yourself*; whatever you do, there is another, alternative you standing invisibly to one side, observing, evaluating, remembering.[24]

The pleasure, the voluptuousness of betrayal thus seems to lie in an infinite production of selves—in a promiscuity of selves. The person who betrays knowingly always plays at least three roles. First, he is his own puppet master, displaying a number of different versions of himself in the field and on the stage, according to the script he is called on to interpret. Second, he is the puppet interpreting the role. In his third role he is the observer—he is his own audience.

His enjoyment lies in the simultaneous management of these different roles, not in succession, but at one and the same time. The betrayer becomes something other than himself, but he also always remains himself. The pleasure of the promiscuity of the multiple self lies in observation—self-observation. There is a hint of voyeurism in the betrayer who is constantly watching himself, observing himself. The betrayer needs an audience before which to perform his betrayal and his deceits, but he himself is always part of that audience.

In the case of betrayal, the voluptuous pleasure of looking at oneself becomes one of watching oneself become another and inducing other people to trust themselves to a pure image. The alternation between creativity and rigor, fantasy and lucidity, and the need to draw a fine line between a spontaneous, improvised performance and keeping to the script—which has to be kept in mind so as to avoid disclosure or contradiction—give the betrayer a thrill that no other form of experience can duplicate. Someone who betrays and is discovered is often a weary gambler, an actor who tosses away his mask. He wants to be discovered, perhaps because he is no longer satisfied by the voluptuous pleasure of betrayal, or perhaps because it is becoming all too enthralling.

2

Living with Betrayal

And in a flash of illumination she saw her whole life dominated by this inexplicable, unremitting betrayal that one commits in every instant, by cutting loose from oneself without knowing why and nevertheless sensing in it an ultimate, inexhaustible tenderness far removed from conscious thought, a tenderness through which one is more immediately linked with oneself than with any of one's actions.
«ROBERT MUSIL, *"The Perfecting of a Love"*»

The Unpredictability of Betrayal

Hannah Arendt states in *The Human Condition* that action is unpredictable because it arises from the "darkness of the human heart"—from the fact that every individual is unreliable because unable to guarantee today what will happen tomorrow—and from our common inability to predict the consequences of an action within a community of equals in which all have a like capacity for action and freedom to act. As Arendt puts it: "Man's inability to rely upon himself or to have complete faith in himself (which is the same thing) is the price human beings pay for freedom; and the impossibility of remaining unique masters of what they do, of knowing its consequences and relying upon the future, is the price they pay for plurality and reality, for the joy of inhabiting together with others a world whose reality is guaranteed for each by the presence of all."[1]

The joy of being with the other in everyday life and the reality founded on intersubjectivity are open to the risk of the unpredictable, hence of betrayal. Arendt stresses that this unpredictability refers not only to the other but also to ourselves, and that no one can say what tomorrow will bring, nor how we will behave in the future. Uncertainty and unpredictability are a part of human action not only thanks to the "darkness of the human heart" but also because no action exists that is not conditioned by the actions of others and that in turn conditions those actions. I can swear to what I will be and what I will do tomorrow, but I always have to take into account that I may change my project; and my plans may be thrown off course or reshaped by the avoidable interference of actions by others. The joy of living with others can lead to both cooperation and betrayal.

This is the fate of Joseph Conrad's Razumov.[2] He mistakenly believes that he can be the one and only master of his life and guide his future along a certain path, but just as soon as another person crosses that path, all definitions lose their clarity. The monotonous flow of Razumov's life is interrupted by the sudden appearance of Hadlin, a student revolutionary who takes refuge in Razumov's house after unsuccessfully attempting a politically motivated assassination. When Hadlin confides in Razumov, thus investing trust in him, all of Razumov's plans for leading a tranquil life and all his dreams of a career as a state functionary vanish. The irruption in his life of young Hadlin, a person almost unknown to him, obliges Razumov to make choices he never could have predicted. For him, honoring the revolutionary's expectation of trust by helping him to flee signifies betrayal of his own self and his own dreams—embarking on a life course contrary to the one he had in mind. On the other hand, dishonoring an unsolicited trust by denouncing Hadlin to the police would mean committing a betrayal. In order to resolve this dilemma, Razumov is forced to redefine himself, his principles, and his values, and to reformulate his definition of betrayal. For there to be betrayal, there must be a moral tie, and he has never established ties of any sort with Hadlin. Through this redefinition of himself and of betrayal, Razumov arrives at a decision to turn the student over to the police.

But even though, according to Razumov's own definition, "all a man can betray is his conscience"—and in fact he does not betray Hadlin, with whom he has no ties and to whom he has no commitment—his encounter with the young revolutionary will change his life.[3] Tragically, during the course of Conrad's story Razumov becomes a police informant in spite of himself. He will betray the trust that others place in him and he will play the betrayer's role precisely because one day Hadlin had chosen him as the person most worthy of his trust. Paradoxically, Hadlin's ill-considered gesture of trust creates for Razumov a destiny as a betrayer. Hadlin's unpredictable gesture gives rise to an equally unpredictable destiny for Razumov.

In a theory of social action based on intersubjectivity such as Hannah Arendt's, each individual acts, always and exclusively, in relation to others and to their acts. This means that no one is ever just the "doer" but is always also the one on whom others' actions are reflected: "To do and to suffer are like opposite sides of the same coin, and the story that an act starts is composed of its consequent deeds and sufferings."[4]

The consequences of action are limitless because every act occurs in a *medium* and prompts a chain reaction, thus putting a new process into motion. Because, according to Arendt, action affects other human beings who are capable of acting in their turn, reactions to such acts are never simple responses, but rather new acts with their own reasons for being that affect others. Human beings are inevitably linked to one another, and no act takes place in isolation, without any effect on others: "The smallest act in the most limited circumstances bears the seed of the same boundlessness, because one deed, and sometimes one word, suffices to change every constellation."[5]

Being with others creates both the possibility of action and its risks. If no human being is ever totally isolated and no gesture or act is ever exclusively the work of one person, how can there be a subject who is intrinsically a betrayer or a subject who is intrinsically the betrayed?

Who can predict betrayal? In Shakespeare's play of the same name, Coriolanus refuses to observe the rules and the rites of the Roman republic by seeking the favor of the Roman people through its tribunes, and his refusal is repaid by insults. This is enough to make the great general feel that he has been betrayed and to induce him to abandon a Rome in which he no longer feels himself appreciated or recognized. Rome, for which he has so often and so generously fought, can no longer be his homeland. How could Coriolanus have predicted, in the happy days of his glory when he defended Rome from its enemies, that one day he would betray its people? How could he have imagined that it would be precisely other Romans who would bring him around to that betrayal? Or that he would be the one to pass over to the side of the Volscians?

Coriolanus's astonishment at finding himself on the side of the enemy, against Rome, leads him to reflect on the unpredictability of action, the impossibility of pinning every act down to a coherent explanation, and the complexity and contradictory nature of being with others. It had been the love and pride he had felt in taking part in an entity called a "homeland" that had made him the most determined defender of Rome. But that same "taking part in," that same "being with others," was what made him a traitor. As he waits outside the Volscian general's house in Antium, Coriolanus, "in mean apparel, disguise'd," exclaims bitterly:

> O world, thy slippery turns! Friends now fast sworn,
> Whose double bosoms seem to wear one heart,
> Whose hours, whose bed, whose meal and exercise
> Are still together, who twin, as 'twere, in love
> Unseparable, shall within this hour,
> On a dissension of a doit, break out
> To bitterest enmity; so, fellest foes,
> Whose passions and whose plots have broke their sleep
> To take the one the other, by some chance,
> Some trick not worth an egg, shall grow dear friends
> And interjoin their issues. So with me:
> My birth-place hate I, and my love's upon
> This enemy town. I'll enter. If he slay me,

He does fair justice; if he give me way,
I'll do his country service.

«*Coriolanus*, 4.4.13–27; Bevington, 1365»

In a theory of action based on intersubjectivity, betrayal never arises out of the simple will of a subject, but is instead always the result of complex and unpredictable relations and interactions. Every action puts into motion not only more or less unpredictable reactions but also unforeseen actions, and it contributes to weaving other and new threads into the web of intersubjectivity. But in order for us to speak of betrayal, the belonging and the sharing need to be not only founded ontologically in intersubjectivity but also concretely rooted in relations, relationships, and interactions in which the individuals involved willingly and reciprocally establish pacts—explicit or implicit—of loyalty and trust. Human beings are free, but at the same time they are always part of a history that is perpetually *in fieri*—in the process of coming into being—and that we all create together. Despite unpredictability, we continue to act in common and to trust one another. Even though we know that promises, pacts, and treaties can be broken, we persist in forging interpersonal bonds: we do so necessarily, as we could not even imagine our future otherwise.

According to Arendt, promises function as "islands of security" in an "ocean of uncertainty." As one of "action's predicaments," they turn the future into something like the present as they attempt to bring solace to "the darkness of each man's lonely heart" and establish connections and relations among humankind.[6] She notes elsewhere that, as Nietzsche suggests, promises constitute a sort of memory of the will; they form networks and drag humans out of their isolation and bestial nature; they are at the base of the possibility of entering into relations with others.[7] But the very fact of drawing up pacts or exchanging promises that link people together introduces the possibility of rupture, abandonment, and betrayal.

If it is true that promises, implicit or explicit, force people out of isolation, it is also true that new promises are ready to take the place of the old ones, and that new ties substitute for old ones.

This is the risk of sharing a space whose confines can never be protected or patrolled tightly enough to prevent flight toward "a world elsewhere." Both the need for promises and the possibility of breaking them are an integral part of intersubjectivity. Yet we must act "as if" the promises and pacts could never be broken, "as if" trust could never be disappointed.

Whereas loyalty between individuals or between the individual and society is an expected part of ordinary knowledge, betrayal—although an integral part of life in society—arrives unexpectedly and is always a break in routine. Betrayal is an event that is at once possible and unexpected, but loyalty is normally—in fact, always—expected. We could not seriously contemplate taking part in any sort of association—from the couple or the group to society at large—if we expected it to bring betrayal, not loyalty. Our social being is founded on implicit and explicit pacts of loyalty and reciprocal trust. Loyalty between the individual and the membership group, society, or the state is a given; it is a part of ordinary expectations and is lodged deep within each one of us. But precisely because loyalty and trust are integral parts of social life, so is the betrayal that constitutes their other face. As social beings we take trust and loyalty for granted, but we know, with varying degrees of lucidity, that betrayal always lies in wait: we know we can be betrayed, and we also know that we are capable of betraying others. This awareness, which varies with the subjects and the relationships they are involved in, can be transformed into fear, a paralyzing inability to act, distrust, or anxiety, or else it can become habit and seem part of ordinary behavior, something we can live with because we take it to be part of life's risks.

Betrayal can thus be listed, sociologically speaking, among those events that, although part of shared experience, are not felt to be routine events, but are rather seen as rare happenings to be averted. We have confidence in the fact that loyalty is more widespread than betrayal. Because it would be impossible to live with the certainty of betrayal, we become used to considering it as an event that might take place but can be warded off. Since betrayal breaks down symbolic order and is a threat to every form of being together, we equate it with death, and, like death, we continually exorcize it. Just as we learn to live with the idea of death, we learn to live with the idea of betrayal, and just as in our everyday acts we are not paralyzed by the idea of death, we soldier on, trusting in loyalty and brushing aside the idea of betrayal.

Knowing and Not Knowing

The ambivalence that inhabits every individual and marks every interaction can be traced to the fact that being for oneself and being in society, as well as the determination and the need to assert both our individuality and our intersubjectivity, are permeated by reasons and passions, self-interest, and emotions. Rather than preexisting within individuals, independent of relationships they may have established, those reasons and passions are created—made and unmade in encounters with others. We can never predict someone else's behavior where loyalty, trust, or betrayal are concerned. As Simmel writes, the other is a stranger not only because, consciously or unconsciously, he lets us glimpse only what he wants, but also because he never knows himself in depth, and because parts of the self become activated or called into existence by the specific and particular relationships in which we happen to find ourselves. To quote Simmel, "No other object of knowledge can reveal or hide itself in the same way, because no other object modifies its behavior in view of the fact that it is recognized."[8]

The blending of what is known and what is not known of the other, the fact that "human interaction is normally based on the fact that the ideational worlds of men have certain elements in common" and that "all of this is interwoven with elements known only to one of the two," includes an awareness of the impossibility of absolute transparency, not only on the part of the other but also on our own part in confrontation with the other.[9] This condition of uncertainty reinforces the ambivalence of interaction, which continually oscillates between trust and mistrust and between possible loyal behaviors and possible betrayals.

The combined presence, in all of us, of multiple roles not necessarily related to one another by any coherent and transparent process makes the psychic apparatus function in a polylogical manner, not only in extreme pathological situations but also in the everyday experience of "normal" people.[10]

The impossibility of inner transparency and coherence lies within us all, and the communication babel begins in the unconscious. We need not appeal to pathology to see that an integrated personality is harder and harder to achieve: individual complexity and intersubjectivity ensure that no one can ever declare himself totally immune from the risk of betraying or being betrayed.

Once the betrayal has occurred, everything seems clear and simple, and the complex personality of the betrayer is reinterpreted and explained by betrayal—as if a definition on the basis of that negative sign could embrace the entire individual. There is no exhaustive answer to the question, "Why have you betrayed?" unless it is an invitation to confront the complexity and ambivalence of the human being.

"Why did you do it?" a young female writer asks the protagonist of John Banville's *The Untouchable*, referring to his betrayal of his fellow spies. Later in the book he returns to the response he should have given: "I am the answer to her question, the totality of what I am; nothing less will suffice. In the public mind, for the brief period it will entertain, and be entertained by, the thought of me, I am a figure with a single salient feature. Even for those who thought they knew me intimately, everything else I have done or not done has faded to insignificance before the fact of my so-called treachery. While in reality all that I am is all of a piece: all of a piece, and yet broken up into a myriad selves."[11]

The existence of the other and the encounter with the other contain the possibility of betrayal, not always as a deliberate, calculated act, but as a possible defection, a subtraction, an incomprehension, or something unpredictable (as we have seen in the case of Conrad's Razumov and as we shall see in the case of the apostle Peter). Nothing guarantees our comprehension of the other, although it is all too often taken for granted. As Franco La Cecla asserts, it is perhaps only an unexpected misunderstanding that gives us a chance to glimpse someone else in his full

unknowableness and diversity: "Misunderstanding has something to do with the encounter. It is the manifestation of the
'in spite of everything' within the apparent normality of daily
life. It reminds us of the deep structure that regulates our desire
for encounter. The encounter is something unexpected, an appearance of the other in his unexpectedness, in surprise, in the
irreconcilability of his being as I had not expected it and as I
cannot invent it."[12]

Betrayal, which often arises from a misunderstanding or an
unpredictable break in everyday routine, suddenly makes us aware
once more that the other exists not only in relation to ourselves
but also in relation to himself or herself and to many others,
whom we may not know. Betrayal brutally imposes on us the
presence of the other and the other's different being.

Do we have to betray in order to assert our own alterity? Do
we have to be betrayed in order to recognize the alterity of others? No, but if we are aware that the possibility of a gap—a withdrawal, an error—exists, it can help us, not so much to prepare to
be betrayed or to betray but to accept ourselves and others as incomplete and complex beings who elude total definition. An
awareness of the possibility of betrayal destroys the illusion of an
infallible and definitive knowledge of oneself and of the other;
what it affirms instead is a knowledge strewn with errors, ap-
proximations, vagueness, and illusions. Moreover, it is precisely
by reason of that errant awareness that we can open our minds
to change and rethink situations and relations.

From this viewpoint, betrayal is a defeat of ordinary knowledge, of stereotypes, and of false certitudes; it checkmates all that
we thought we knew. However, it also reactivates the mind, inviting it to wake up to the challenge of something that seems
unequivocally unknown, ungraspable, and unpredictable.

Betrayal is relational not only because it involves two subjects
but because it arises out of an action, a communication, or a feeling that moves incessantly from one person to the other. In betrayal there is always a flow, a happening that passes from the one
to the other through an intermediate space, never well defined,

in which actions meet. That shared space is made of trust and expectations, but also of ambiguity and complicity; in it each projects images and desires onto the other, and both collaborate actively to shape and maintain the interaction, interpreting its meaning in ways that are not necessarily concordant.

The subjects send one another images of how they would like to be judged: A communicates to B, consciously or unconsciously, his or her evaluative criteria and standards for accepting the other. B seeks to live up to those criteria and sends A an image of himself or herself congruent with them, but B also communicates criteria and standards, to which A seeks to conform. This creates a reciprocal acceptance and a mutual trust between the two subjects that is based more on their reciprocal requests for congruent responses to their own criteria of evaluation than on their expectations. Thus both parties tend to take on a different mask and a different comportment according to their interactions and to what I call "local situations"—specific situations located in the *hic et nunc* of space and time. This game of expectations, projections, illusions, and misunderstandings creates the space in which the encounter takes place, but it is also the space of the illusion of knowing the other.

Being for Oneself; Being for the Other

By nature, individuals are born neither altruistic nor egoistic, neither loyal nor traitorous, but are at once cooperative and competitive, trusted and untrustworthy. Simmel has shown how the joint presence, within each individual, of cooperation and competitiveness, loyalty and a capacity for betrayal, being for oneself and being within society, lends ambivalence and ambiguity to social interaction. This is what Kant calls "unsociable sociability." We want to be both loyal to and traitorous with the other; we try to satisfy our social being and our being for ourselves. Not every betrayal can be attributed to being for oneself, nor can every loyal act be ascribed to our social being. For example, loyal attitudes and behaviors can arise out of a need to satisfy a self-image as loyal and trustworthy—that is, to ways of trying to realize being for oneself. On the other hand, we can betray to satisfy a request from the group, the community, or the society to which we belong. Betrayals that derive from conflicts of loyalty are an example of this: people betray their best friend in order not to betray their country; they betray their own family in order not to betray a pact with a group of which they are a member.

New loyalties and new memberships often involve the abandonment of old ties, even such strong ties as those between mother and daughter. The will to realize one's own social being can lead to extremely cruel betrayals, and the world of affective connections can seem to us a trap, a prison that holds us back from realizing ourselves and confines us within our small world. It is possible to betray, using realization of our social being in order to satisfy being for oneself. When this happens, the betrayal cannot be attributed solely to the satisfaction of the egoistic part of the self. But because detaching oneself from the world of primary affections and ties is so painful, we need destructive gestures, actions, and words to serve as symbolic proof of the break and the transfer from one membership to another.

In *Il gioco dei Regni*, Clara Sereni describes her mother's harsh treatment of her grandmother. Xenia, Sereni's mother, a militant Communist, has accepted the party's demand that she break off all familial ties, in particular, her tie with her own mother, who in her youth had been an anarchist. Although the older woman suffers from this withdrawal, she accepts it in silence for a number of years. When she learns that Xenia is dying, however, she hastens to her daughter's side. She is rejected again. Xenia permits her mother to administer her medicines and to help her out of bed, but she refuses to speak to her. Even in her dying moments, the daughter confirms her political choice, betraying all affective ties with her mother. Once more rejected and denied, the old mother, speaking to Xenia's husband, a Communist leader who feels pity for her, launches into a desperate tirade:

> Don't worry, I'm used to it. With Xeniuska it has always been this way. God only knows how much I suffered from it, how much I

criticized her rigidity, her shutting me out. When she used to shout at me that I was an ineffectual relic of the past, a little old lady, a uselessly romantic petty bourgeois. And she a totally new woman, because she had the party, because she had you.... To be whole inside the party she tore me to pieces.[13]

Even self-betrayal, which in appearance arises and develops within a single subject and regards only that subject's individuality, is situated within the sociological space constructed by the relations that we maintain with others and by the intersubjectivity that permits us to perceive ourselves as subjects. The idea that we have of ourselves is always in reference to others, because it puts into play shared experiences, choices, values, and behaviors that refer to our social being. Self-betrayal can mean the betrayal of one's own identity and of the image of ourselves that we have constructed freely, not in solitude, but necessarily together with others. We can also choose to betray ourselves or not to do so if we want to avoid betraying the image that others have of us, an image that we have more or less consciously helped to create. The betrayal or nonbetrayal of oneself is also linked to the type of interactions and relations that we have with others and to whether we want to confirm or destroy not only others' expectations of us but also the image that they have of us. Thus self-betrayal as well springs from intersubjectivity.

In his novel *Uno, nessuno e centomila* (*One, No One, and One Hundred Thousand*), Luigi Pirandello portrays the drama of Vitangelo Moscarda, a man faced with an impossible choice between an identity that leaves others out of all consideration and an identity that corresponds to their image of him. Moscarda is forced to betray a part of himself—one among the hundred thousand parts that others see in him—and to betray his multilayered identity. His only option is to be no one, to be a madman, as the one way to live up to what he has discovered to be his true self.[14]

In *Coriolanus*, Shakespeare relates a drama of extreme fidelity to the self. Coriolanus chooses to abandon his homeland so as to avoid betraying his own nature and what he believes in. In a dramatic confrontation with his mother, who begs him to pretend and to flatter the people of Rome, Coriolanus responds:

> . . . I will not do't,
> Lest I surcease to honor mine own truth
> And by my body's action teach my mind
> A most inherent baseness.

> «*Coriolanus*, 3.3.122–25; Bevington, 1360»

Coriolanus prefers to betray the conventions and the rules of republican Rome rather than betray himself, and when the sentence is delivered that condemns him to exile and brands him with the infamous accusation of treason, he chooses another homeland and membership in another community. Although his self is intact, Coriolanus is truly an exile, a man in search of a new affiliation, of "a world elsewhere" where he can be accepted as he is:

> . . . Have the power still
> To banish your defenders, till at length
> Your ignorance, which finds not till it fells,
> Making but reservation of yourselves,
> Still your own foes, deliver you as most
> Abated captives to some nation
> That won you without blows! Despising,
> For you, the city, thus I turn my back.
> There is a world elsewhere.

> «*Coriolanus*, 3.3.131–39; Bevington, 1362»

The "world elsewhere" is the camp of the Volscians, Rome's enemies. If he is not to betray himself, Coriolanus has to pass over to the enemy; he has to consummate his betrayal of his homeland and choose to be fully elsewhere, far from his former community, his affective ties, and his sense of membership. Disowned by his fellow Romans, he has no choice but to seek another world.

3

Betrayal as Everyday Experience

I am not what I am.
«IAGO, *Othello*, 1.1.66; Bevington, 1126 »

Judas and Peter: Two Archetypes

Much of our store of images connected with betrayal and our common knowledge of it are based on the stories of Judas Iscariot and Peter in the Gospel narratives. Beyond the religious significance of these two figures and the theological explanations connected with them (still a topic of lively debate among biblical scholars), their two betrayals stand as examples of the uncertainty that constantly accompanies all human relationships. Both betrayals involve membership in a group, and both reveal the deepseated ambivalence always connected with being part of a We. Judas betrays by revealing what should be kept hidden, while Peter betrays in his denial of Christ.

JUDAS ISCARIOT: THE NEED TO BETRAY
Judas's betrayal of Jesus has become the archetype of all betrayals. In ordinary parlance "Judas" is an epithet synonymous with

"traitor": such expressions as "to play the Judas" and "the kiss of Judas" signify betrayal.

Judas has always been treated as the worst of all betrayers. Dante places him in the most horrifying part of the *Inferno*, the fourth and last section of the frozen lake, Cocytus, where Christ's betrayer is stuck, head down, in Lucifer's mouth. The most terrible punishment imaginable is inflicted on the greatest sinner—to be ground for all eternity between the teeth of the Devil, the traitor angel and the only being more wicked than Judas:

> "That soul up there who suffers most of all,"
> my guide explained, "is Judas Iscariot:
> the one with head inside and legs out kicking."[1]

Judas's act of betrayal has always appeared intolerable, even to those who are not believing Christians, not only because it is Christ who is betrayed but also because Judas sells out friendship, trust, and loyalty for money. For money, Judas has not only betrayed the Master and the Son of God, but a friend with whom he has ties of affection and trust. Some commentators—Mario Brelich among them—have challenged the historical veracity and the internal coherence of the affair: thirty pieces of silver could hardly buy a jar of ointment, and Judas revealed nothing of importance to the priests, who knew very well where Jesus was to be found.[2] Thus it is hardly credible that Judas could have betrayed Jesus for a jar of ointment, nor that the priests would have been willing to pay thirty pieces of silver for information they already had. In "Three Versions of Judas" Jorge Luis Borges has one "Nils Runeberg" note that Judas's act is superfluous: "In order to identify a teacher who preached daily in the synagogue and worked miracles before thousands of men, betrayal by an apostle is unnecessary.'"[3]

More than the motivations for Judas's betrayal, what we need to investigate is the nature of that act and seek to understand what pacts and implicit rules of membership he broke. Above all, Judas's betrayal lies in his revelation of the secret that united the disciples and Jesus, which was the establishment of a new order and the appearance of a new king. Whether he does so thought-lessly, out of a foolish ignorance, or perhaps simply out of pride in having a part in such an extraordinary project, Judas reveals the secrets and rituals of his community. Highly pleased with himself and proud of both his membership in this group and his king, who will soon be the king of all men, Judas does more than deliver (*trādere*) Jesus into the hands of the authorities; he hands over and betrays secrets, and he reveals the profound significance of the group's existence. As Brelich writes, it is Judas's profound faith in the words of Jesus and his conviction that Jesus is the true Messiah that lead Judas to reveal to the priests that Jesus is not just another preacher but a figure much more dangerous to them.[4] William Klassen pursued a similar line of argumentation some years ago, absolving Judas of the accusation of treachery.[5]

The Gospel narrative describes a complex relationship. The actors in this drama are not only Jesus and Judas but also the other eleven apostles, who are part of the same community. Like all groups, the apostles have a joint project: the dissemination of the Gospel and the realization of the divine mission. To be faithful to the Master and to be faithful to the group to which they belong means to work for the realization of common objectives. But if that is the case, to hand over—*trādere*—Jesus to his executioners can be seen as the very act needed for fulfillment of the divine plan that includes his crucifixion. At the Last Supper, when Jesus announces, "One of you will betray me," he is in fact declaring that one of his own apostles, his most beloved disciples, must *necessarily* see to it that the divine will is fulfilled. Jesus is not simply predicting this: because he has faith in his disciples he expects one of them to betray him by handing him over to his executioners.

Without the delivery of Jesus to his enemies—which means without the betrayal of Judas—there could have been no Cruci-fixion, thus no fulfillment of the human role of the Son of God.[6] The fulfillment of God's plan requires the collaboration of all the disciples, each one playing his part. Judas's role will be the most thankless one. He cannot demonstrate his loyalty and faithful-ness to the Master by defending and protecting him; quite the contrary, he must see to it that destiny is realized. Jesus does not ask to be protected but rather to be betrayed and delivered to his enemies. The Gospel narratives report that when the soldiers of the high priest arrive, accompanied by Judas, to arrest Jesus, Peter draws his sword to defend him. But "At that Jesus said to Peter, 'Put your sword back in its sheath. Am I not to drink the cup the Father has given me?'" (John 18:11).

Jesus reproaches Peter for hindering the divine plan. To prevent his betrayal and his delivery would be tantamount to opposing the realization of an outcome in which all the apostles were expected to collaborate. Paradoxically, Peter's courageous and caring gesture may be dictated by loyalty and love, but it is a betrayal of the common goal.

The true betrayal of Jesus would thus have been to oppose the realization of the divine plan, to misconstrue the goal of the community formed by the Master and his apostles. Paradoxically, the one who betrays Jesus by handing him over to his enemies is acting as Jesus expects him to. Judas's betrayal of Jesus can thus be considered necessary. This interpretation has a validity and a logic within the theological explanation of free will, which reads Judas's betrayal as a necessary act, but also as the result of Judas's own free will. Within the relations among Jesus, Judas, and the other apostles we can therefore trace a series of internal processes that lead to betrayal. We can hypothesize that Judas may have had an unconscious desire to disappoint Jesus's expectations; that the master-disciple relationship may always have contained a degree of ambivalence; that Judas, because of that ambivalence, may have wanted to assert his own autonomy, separate himself from the Master, and kill the symbolic father; or that he may have wanted to play the protagonist, steal the scene and be the one who makes a sensational gesture that will long be remembered. Judas was a member of the disciples' group, but that affiliation did not occupy his entire identity: he may have yearned for something else, even for "a world elsewhere." Perhaps he wanted to be the one to reveal prematurely to the world what was about to take place, to narrate and transmit it (and we should not forget that *trādere* also means to transmit), and to use narrative to seem the craftsman of an extraordinary event.

Ambivalence, narcissism, a desire to take the role of protagonist, may perhaps explain Judas's act from a secular point of view. His betrayal remains unpardonable within tradition and the common store of images precisely because it developed within a community, within a We. It does not do away with Jesus, but with Judas's fellow disciples; it sweeps away all trust in loyalty and friendship. Judas's betrayal is unexpected; it is a disquieting act because it shows that everywhere and at all times there may be someone capable of betrayal, for a complex of reasons and passions that are hard to understand. Volumes have been written about why Judas betrayed Jesus and about the theological significance of his act, as the thick documentation cited in Klassen's book testifies. What is most interesting from our point of view, however, is that no group can ever claim itself immune to betrayal, not even a community such as the twelve apostles, whose every member had been chosen and had freely agreed to join the group. Thus not only can no one ever claim to be certain of his own acts but there are no membership groups so strong that betrayal cannot arise in their midst. From the viewpoint of a phenomenology of betrayal, what fascinates us in the story of Judas's betrayal of Jesus is precisely the feeling of uncertainty, imminent danger, and unease that seems to strike all of the apostles. When Jesus flatly states, during the Last Supper, that one of them will betray him, not a one of his disciples can openly and confidently state, "Not I." Rather, each of them tests his own fragility, perhaps becoming aware of being capable of betrayal: "In the course of the meal he said, 'I assure you, one of you is about to betray me.' Distressed at this, they began to say to him one after another, 'Surely it is not I, Lord?'" (Matthew 26:21–22).

That question, which seems more turned inward toward themselves than toward their master, and that self-doubt ("Surely it is not I?") contain the full drama of what is about to take place, but above all of the drama of being with others, of not ever being totally sure of one's own self in respect to others. It will turn out to be Judas who will bear the burden of the glaringly obvious betrayal by turning Jesus over to the chief priests, but the other apostles experience serious doubts about themselves. In fact, when their Master is arrested, they all flee, abandoning him to his fate.

But why do the Gospels narrate this betrayal, thus "making" it happen? If it is clear from the perspective of Christian doctrine that Christ must die, from a secular viewpoint we still need to ask why that death, for all its necessity for the realization of the divine plan, must take place through betrayal. Why don't the Gospels simply narrate the imprisonment, condemnation, and crucifixion of the Master, a series of events that occurred rather frequently at the time to preachers who were accused of creating public disorder? Why did the Gospels need to set up and recount a betrayal? What narrative demands required betrayal—required a Judas? There are probably two levels of motivations here, one within the type of narrative that transmits the story of Judas to us, the other linked to betrayal as a type of human experience.

The Gospel narratives relate the life of Jesus, but along the way they tell us a great deal about everyday life at the time; not only a valuable source of religious teaching, they make up an extremely important text of social history. They tell us about trades and crafts, customs, and ways of thinking; about people's anxieties and social relations; about vices and virtues. Betrayal cannot be omitted in this detailed reconstruction of everyday life in society. Betrayal is a part of all the great narratives: we need only think of the *Odyssey* and the *Iliad*, in which both men and gods betray and are betrayed by one another. In short, betrayal will be present wherever everyday life is narrated and wherever there is an account of relationships and social interactions.

But precisely why must Christ be betrayed? Probably it is because being betrayed, undergoing an experience that is both so painful and so common, makes Jesus a man like all men. His humanity becomes plausible only when it is based in intersubjectivity, anchored by an experience of the ambiguity and ambivalence typical of all interaction—exposure to the risks of being with the other, hence exposure to the risk of betrayal. For the

Son of God to become completely an earthly man, he must not only die like all other human beings but must experience all the pain and suffering of human life; he must know not only physical suffering but also the pain of being betrayed by someone near and dear to him, by one of his beloved disciples. He must go through the experience of abandonment, be thrown into the world, know doubt and torment, and learn that even the Father is capable of betrayal and abandonment.[7]

"My God, my God, why have you forsaken me?" Jesus cries out on the cross. It is that heartfelt cry protesting an abandonment that seems the ultimate and intolerable betrayal that makes him wholly human, wholly a being who, like all beings, may be abandoned and betrayed—even by his own father and those closest to him.

To become man implies going through the experience of abandonment and betrayal and knowing the ambivalence of being with others. What Judas did, which is necessary for the realization of the Master's own words, is also emblematic of the impossibility of avoiding betrayal in human interactions. To live with others means to join them in passing through the insidious dark space where betrayal is always possible. The person who is betrayed feels abandoned; the betrayer discovers his disloyalty and ambivalence. This is the experience Judas goes through as he discovers that he is a traitor, capable of inflicting pain, of wounding, even killing. It is that same terrible experience that makes Jesus a man. Borges writes that Christ's becoming wholly man cannot be limited to the Crucifixion; rather, Jesus chooses to pass through the most terrible of human experiences, which is not that of being betrayed, but rather that of betraying: "To limit what He underwent to the agony of one afternoon on the cross is blasphemous. . . . God made Himself totally a man but a man to the point of infamy, a man to the point of reprobation and the abyss. To save us, He could have chosen any one of the destinies which make up the complex web of history; He could have been Alexander or Pythagoras or Rurik or Jesus; He chose the vilest destiny of all: He was Judas."[8]

In the story of Judas, betrayal appears as a necessary, ineluctable form of experience: it springs from the ambiguity and complexity of intersubjectivity, from being and not being fully present, and from the sense of affiliation and withdrawal that are typical of all encounters with the other. In this perspective, the suicide of Judas takes on a different meaning as well. It can be interpreted not only as being motivated by an unbearable feeling of guilt but also as a sign of Judas's inability to tolerate his own internal ambiguity. Judas the Betrayer does not want to betray his relationship with the Master totally; he cannot disavow the friendship, faith, and respect that had united them. For that reason he cannot pretend that nothing had happened but instead must take responsibility for what he has done. Judas chooses suicide, not as a final act of reparation, but as an extreme gesture of loyalty and recognition of the relationship that he had had with Jesus. Judas hangs himself because he has achieved the goal of his betrayal and realized its meaning: he does not want to betray Jesus further by forgetting all that had taken place between them. His suicide is a way of maintaining his relationship with Jesus even as he recognizes that his betrayal was necessary and takes responsibility for it.

Deliberately ignoring his own internal ambiguity and the acts that followed from it could only be possible through yet another betrayal, a self-betrayal to silence the unacceptable portions of the self. Instead, Judas chooses to accept his own ambivalence, to take on and recognize the darkest parts of himself, even if he lacks the strength to tolerate them. By hanging himself he betrays neither himself nor—in the final analysis—Jesus. Judas had betrayed Jesus by handing him over to his enemies, but he did not disavow him, and he did not disavow himself.

The suicide of Judas is an assumption of responsibility, an act that provides an insight into a complex and suffering man, not just a traitorous betrayer.

PETER: THE BANALITY OF BETRAYAL

Peter provides another archetype of betrayal, but it is one that has been transmitted with a degree of tolerance, almost absolution.

Why? Simply because Peter was pardoned by the Lord and went on to be the founder of the church? Is the benevolence shown to Peter to be attributed to "political" reasons alone? To a fear of de-legitimizing the father of the church? Or is Peter's betrayal more tolerable because we can identify with it more easily, given that we are capable of replicating it every day of our lives?

Peter is a simple man, a fisherman, not a man of letters or an intellectual like John or Luke. More than the others, he is an embodiment of human frailty; he displays a lack of self-awareness and harbors a dark area concealing those parts of ourselves we do not want to admit to. Precisely because Peter embodies all of this, he becomes a symbol for and the emblem of the small everyday betrayals that we are all capable of committing.

Peter betrays by placing himself for a moment outside of the We, outside of the membership circle. Why? Out of cowardice, ignorance, or opportunism, but also simply by chance, because of the contradictions inherent in the mind and the ambiguities of the human condition; because we are not always aware, we are all incoherent, and we are dragged along and changed by every interaction.

In this sense, Peter's betrayal becomes more emblematic of the human condition than Judas's. Peter betrays for no true reason, without motivation or predisposition. Jesus's premonition, "I tell you, Peter, the cock will not crow today until you have three times denied that you know me" (Luke 22:34), seems to Peter both intolerable and unjust, and it throws him into despair. But it is Peter, who has sworn to be loyal to Jesus to the death, who will be forced to become acquainted with his dark side and his disloyalty.

Because Peter's denial is so unexpected, it contains all of the complexity of the individual and of intersubjectivity, to the point that we can take it as a metaphor for the ambiguity of our being with others and for our own ambiguity.

Jesus can foretell Peter's betrayal, not so much thanks to divine foresight as because of a human awareness of the irreducible complexity of humankind and the way we hide ourselves from both our own selves and others. Peter's betrayal shows that not only can we always be betrayed but that we ourselves can always be the betrayers. Not only can we not swear to someone else's behavior except out of blind trust or as an act of faith but we can never sincerely and honestly swear to our own behavior, because no one can predict how much and in what ways encounters with others will change us, nor what we will create together.

Every encounter with the other brings to light new and unknown parts of ourselves. Every encounter is marked by risk, because we are never the same. Peter swears fidelity to Jesus in good faith because at that moment he views himself as loyal and faithful. But when he finds himself in another context, immersed in other interactions, he discovers previously unknown parts of himself. He is no longer the Peter of the Peter-Jesus relationship but also a Peter who is alone and frightened in a confrontation with the Roman soldiers and the Galileans. The possibility and the risk of betrayal slips between the cracks of also being other, of even being many others, or being unable to be wholly present.

This is how Peter, the faithful disciple, denies three times that he knows Jesus, denies his affiliation, and betrays the We, almost unconsciously placing himself outside of it. That lack of awareness provides, if not a justification for Peter's betrayal, at least a degree of acceptability for it. His betrayal is unsought and unwilled; it springs from the hazards and the daily routine of life; it is a betrayal that permits us to view him with compassion. Still, there remains the drama of his triple "No." Discovering that betrayal lurks within us almost "as a natural act" is just as tragic and painful as to have betrayed deliberately to achieve an end.

The tears to which Peter abandons himself when he realizes that he has denied Jesus three times are not so much the tears of the guilty as they are the tears of all who discover that they are fragile, ambiguous, and multiple.

The Thousand Faces of Betrayal: Elizabeth I and the Earl of Essex

The story of the tempestuous relationship between Elizabeth I of England and Robert Devereux, Earl of Essex, is a succession of betrayals that ends tragically with the earl's decapitation.[9] That was the punishment decreed by the queen after Essex's failed attempt to stir up the population of London to rebel against her and to remove her from the throne. This extreme betrayal capped a crescendo of small betrayals of every type: of role, of everyday rituals, of both parties' expectations regarding the other's behavior.[10]

Past a certain point, nothing between Elizabeth and the Earl of Essex worked according to the rules or according to expectations. Every move, gesture, or word on the part of one of them inflicted a wound on the other, insinuated a suspicion, and invited doubts and predictions of betrayal.

Before they reached the point of mistrusting one another's sentiments, Elizabeth and Essex lost faith in the other's behavior within their everyday encounters and interactions, both public and private. Gestures, words, and the observance of rituals became completely unpredictable, and each was aware that betrayal can come on any terrain: power, love, game playing, encounter, or communication. As was true of all of Elizabeth's love affairs, their relationship, although long lasting, was always precarious, as she never gave herself fully to any of her lovers. Everyone at court was aware of their relationship, and not even Essex's most determined enemies dared attack him in the presence of the queen. Thus Elizabeth and Robert Devereux made up a We, both in their private moments and in public.

From the beginning, their relationship was marked by fluctuations on both sides in their being fully present or not. Essex was an earl, and even though he was the queen's favorite, he remained her subject. Elizabeth, on the other hand, was both the queen of England and in love with Essex. Theirs was a relationship imbued with ambiguity, with mutual expectations, with power inequalities, and with both love and fear, trust and suspicion. It was also hemmed in by rules, spoken and unspoken.

Essex was the queen's favorite for a number of years. She was by then sixty years old and had never been a great beauty, and he was the only one who amused her and made her feel loved and seductive. She was attracted to the earl, a man much younger than she, by his charm, his passionate nature, his intensity, his impetuosity, and his heedlessness. Elizabeth thought she could count on him as a faithful lover and loyal subject; she expected him to know how to play the often contradictory roles of lover and subject. She expected fidelity, loyalty, and obedience, but also admiration, love, and passion.

These were extremely high expectations, inscribed within a double framework of the rigid rules of the court and the more indistinct rules of a love relationship. The coexistence of these two quite different and even contradictory local situations within the same time and space made each of the parties somewhat diffident regarding role expectations. Elizabeth expected the earl to behave according to the rules of the court and the implicit rules of the amorous relationship. Essex's charms, which she found so fascinating, kept her suspended in an indefinable anxiety, both as a woman and as queen. In order to trust Essex, the queen needed ongoing verification that he understood the rules of the court and the rules of love and was competent in both roles.

How long would the young and restless earl continue to be at her side? To what extent could she impose her power on him as queen and as a woman?

For his part, Essex was sincerely in love with Elizabeth. He admired her, esteemed her, and had sworn eternal loyalty to her, not only because she was queen of England but because she was *his* queen. But this was precisely the problem: Elizabeth was not only *his* queen and his lover, she was *the* queen, the most powerful figure in the kingdom, who held life-and-death power over all her subjects, Essex included. Essex must have had to force himself to remember that the woman he loved and by whom he was loved nonetheless remained the queen of England. Elizabeth might show him favors and grant him many privileges, but she could also decide otherwise. Essex was in her power, and he could be rejected as a lover and disappointed in his ambitions. This means that Essex oscillated between gratitude and loyalty and fears and anxieties.

What did Essex expect of Elizabeth? That she act with the audacity, the courage, and the nobility proper to a sovereign, qualities that had attracted and enchanted him. He expected her to play her role as sovereign well, but also to act and govern according to his beliefs and desires and use her power in his favor—to let herself be guided, counseled, and influenced. Essex wanted Elizabeth, as a woman, to submit to him; he expected her to play the role of queen, but also that of a woman in love. He wanted to test how much the queen loved him and how much he could influence her, to what extent he could seduce her, bring her closer to him, and induce her to act in his favor.

This means that Essex, too, had dual and contradictory expectations. He was well aware that Elizabeth would lose prestige and authority if she showed herself too pliant and too much under his influence in public. If his position as the queen's favorite was to gain public recognition, he knew that the queen must act at all times as a sovereign. He was also well aware that they could make a public display of their relationship only if they staged a performance of it that was acceptable according to the rules of the court. Before the court, which was their audience, Elizabeth and Essex formed what Erving Goffman calls a theatrical team; as such, they had to be careful to play to one another and not disappoint their spectators, who expected to see them play the roles of queen and subject.

Role expectations are rendered even more complex here by the fact that Elizabeth and Essex were a woman and a man, hence had gender expectations of one another. Although a dominating and autonomous woman, Elizabeth, like all women of her time and station, expected respect, discretion, dedication, protection, gentleness, and gallantry of a man. Essex, as a man of his time, expected docility, submission, fidelity, esteem, and unconditioned admiration.

Both Elizabeth and Essex were playing multiple roles that are difficult to disentangle. Their relationship never provided a local situation in which one role could give way to another or in which either of them could choose one role and drop the others. Even in their most intimate moments Elizabeth could not resign from her role as queen of England, nor could Essex escape his role of subject. Their every interaction took place on a mined field. There were too many—and often contradictory—norms to be respected; there were too many roles to be played simultaneously. Their interactions shifted between certainty and uncertainty, rigid rules and improvisations. Conflict lurked everywhere in their relationship, ready to explode at the first misstep. That opportunity came with the war against the Catholics (supported by Spain) in Ireland, a war that dragged on unevenly for years and eventually swallowed up the wealth and the forces of the kingdom. Up to that point Elizabeth and Essex still trusted one another as actors in the same play and as partners in a We. They were sure that whatever happened and even if one rule or another was not respected neither would attack their ability to interact. Both had confidence that their We would not come under assault, no matter how tempestuous their discussions, encounters, and relations might be.

During a discussion regarding the expedition to Ireland, however, the rules of interaction were abruptly broken, with both Elizabeth and Essex betraying their mutual expectations and changing what both had thought to be an encounter and discussion in full respect of the rules, court relations, and their relationship into a confrontation.

The Lord Deputy Borough, viceroy of Ireland, had died suddenly, and Tyrone, the leader of the rebels in Ulster, had reopened hostilities. A new viceroy had to be named immediately. Essex wanted the post of governor of Ireland to go to Sir George Carew, one of his family's followers, but Elizabeth was determined to entrust the charge to Sir William Knollys. "At that the Queen roundly declared that, say what he would, Knollys should go. Essex, overcome with irritation, contemptuous in look and gesture, turned his back upon her." Essex was thus guilty of a severe infraction of the rules covering the behavior of a subject toward his queen. Elizabeth, infuriated by this insult and by what seemed to her a betrayal of role expectations, "instantly boxed his ears. 'Go to the devil!' she cried, flaring with anger."[11]

With that act and that slap, Elizabeth instantly broke more than one rule. Essex was a subject of hers, to be sure, but he was still an earl and a male. A queen does not slap an earl, and a woman does not slap a man: these were the rules of her dual role of woman and queen. With that act, performed before the court, Elizabeth humiliated Essex as a noble and disavowed him as a lover; she abandoned and betrayed him. Her slap not only broke the rules and violated the order of their interaction, it also publicly betrayed her relationship with Essex by withdrawing from it in the most ostentatious manner. By openly showing an irritation that must remain hidden as part of her backstage life, she revealed to her audience that, when all was said and done, she could treat Essex like any one of her subjects. Elizabeth betrayed the We of Elizabeth and Essex, leaving the earl alone and humiliated and stripping him of any possible role to play.

At that point, Essex lost control of himself, hastily seeking another role—not the part of the faithful and loyal subject and lover, but that of the young male, offended and infuriated and capable of revolt and of betraying his queen. Essex responded to Elizabeth's public betrayal and abandonment with an even greater betrayal and disavowal: "The mad young man completely lost his temper, and, with a resounding oath, clapped his hand to his sword. 'This is an outrage,' he shouted in his sovereign's face, 'that I will not put up with. I would not have borne it from your father's hands.'"[12]

We need to look a bit more closely at the earl's behavior and his words. When Essex was slapped, he lost face in the eyes of the public (that is, the court) and felt himself betrayed. Abruptly ejected from the Elizabeth-Essex We, he no longer had any reason to maintain their joint performance. Betrayed in their interaction and their relationship, he in turn betrayed the queen.

The words, "This is an outrage that . . . I would not have borne . . . from your father's hands" contain something more than a response to a terrible offence. They represent an attack, an aggression, and a total disavowal of Elizabeth as both his queen and his lover. The message his words convey is "I am the Earl of Essex; not even a king can offend me, and I will certainly not take it from a woman."

Essex disavows Elizabeth both as queen of England and as queen of his heart. By his implicit demand, "Who are you to dare so much?" he too betrays the double We of queen-subject and Elizabeth-Essex.

In an instant there was no more We: the We that had been formed by the relationship and that was the pretext for that encounter had been wiped out by their interaction there. The frame that contained and defined the scene had now been torn away in too many places; the mutual disavowals and betrayals that took place in a swift chain of moves and countermoves forced a redefinition of the two protagonists' roles in this drama, and they now had to prepare for a new performance. Essex had let his emotions get the better of him; by losing his self-control he put himself out of the picture.

Goffman calls this loss of control "flooding out": "Under certain circumstances the individual may allow his manner to be inundated by a flow of affect that he no longer makes a show of concealing. . . . [The individual] radically alters his general support of the interaction; he is momentarily 'out of play.' Since the individual has been active in some social role up to this time, sustaining the frame around the encounter, his flooding out constitutes one type of 'breaking the frame.'"[13]

First Essex and then Elizabeth failed to play the expressive role appropriate to interaction; they both "flooded out," giving free rein to their emotions of anger, pride, and rage. They betrayed public expectations as well—in this instance, those of the court, which was prepared for a very different performance. The court remained silent and disoriented; without a playbook they found they had no role to play. Goffman claims that when an individual floods out, that behavior is often deliberately ignored by the others so that the performance (and the interaction) can go on as if nothing had happened. In the case of Elizabeth and Essex, however, the flooding out was so major that it could not be ignored, and in fact it produced other floods by contagion. The other actors in this drama did their best not to maintain the frame but to break it up; it was as if each had chosen a part of it to destroy and concentrated on that point. The techniques for limiting the damage of flooding out that Goffman cites failed to work in this case: the frame had been broken at too many points, leaving the performers bare on stage. All masks dropped simultaneously, and new ones could not be slipped on so hastily. It is in this sense that this incident represents a betrayal of an interaction and not just a failure to respect the rules.

Something happened in the scene that we have just examined that sapped the relationship and made it impossible for them to pursue the encounter. Here it is not the case that betrayal of the relationship is reflected in the betrayal of the interaction; rather, the betrayal of the relationship occurred simultaneously with the betrayal of the interaction. Elizabeth and Essex lost mutual trust on the level of their interaction, but also on that of their relationship.

From that moment on, each viewed the other as discredited, and on both sides role expectations became loaded with distrust and fear. After that incident, both the audience—the court—and the two actors prepared for a new drama: treasonous betrayal.

Also from that moment on, the two protagonists took very seriously their respective expectations of betrayal, precisely because they had seen each other withdraw all support from their joint performance. Henceforth, each would imagine the other in the act of betrayal. All mutual trust was now impossible; the faith in the other as an actor adequate to a social performance vanished along with the certainty of being a team, of forming a We. Now Elizabeth and Essex were afraid of each other: they were both aware that they might be betrayed and were capable of betrayal. Neither was trustworthy in the other's eyes; each had discredited the other.

After that incident, each of them reinterpreted their love story and their allegiance in the light of their reciprocal betrayal. In a letter addressed to Elizabeth, Essex wrote: "When I remember that your Majesty hath, by the intolerable wrong you have done both me and yourself, not only broken all laws of affection, but done against the honour of your sex, I think all places better than that where I am, and all dangers well undertaken, so I might retire myself from the memory of my false, inconstant and beguiling pleasures. . . . I was never proud, till your Majesty sought to make me too base."[14]

Here Essex, like all who feel themselves betrayed, repudiates everything that happened before the betrayal; he disavows his former self and the relationship; he rereads every gesture and every word as deceitful. The earl can no longer recognize himself in an individual who was so weak as to allow himself to be manipulated and deceived by a woman. To redefine himself and win back his own self-respect, Essex needed to attribute all that had occurred to an inattentive and false self.

Essex accuses the queen of having forced him to place his hand on his sword so as to avoid losing face and to maintain his role as a male and an earl. He was both unable and unwilling to appear "base," and, even if the person who had offended him was the queen of England, his social role obliged him to react and mend his wounded pride: "I was never proud, till your Majesty sought to make me too base."

Not reacting to the queen's slap would have brought on a loss of honor and self-esteem, but it also would have earned him discredit and disapproval from his public. However, his excessive reaction, his hand moving to his sword, placed him out of the game and discredited him anyway. Essex felt himself profoundly betrayed: Elizabeth had left him no way out, no part to play, no role. The queen had checkmated him. What was Essex to do? Essex punished the queen by denying her his company, retiring to his castle in voluntary exile.

Although Elizabeth missed Essex immensely, she was now living in a state of high alert because she knew that the earl was capable of not respecting the rules and of revolting against her. And what if his fury and his pride should push him to high treason? Driven by such doubts, the queen sought proofs to confirm her suspicions. When suspicion creeps in and trust shrinks, all willingness to believe in the other vanishes. The perverse nature of distrust makes it feed on itself, nourished by proofs that it itself constructs.

At this point Elizabeth felt some bitterness, but she was ready for the earl's betrayal because she had already internalized the idea of it in her mind. For his part, Essex, in a series of ill-considered acts, lived up to the queen's expectations of him, cooperating with her to construct his role as a traitor. Once the double We of queen-earl and Elizabeth-Essex and all previous role expectations had been betrayed, Elizabeth and Essex actively collaborated to fulfill their reciprocal expectations of betrayal. The only thing missing was a new drama to perform.

Another expedition to Ireland, led by Essex, was going very badly, and insistent voices confirmed the queen's suspicion that the earl was in fact working to reinforce his own power. For his part, Essex felt himself watched, disapproved of, and abandoned. His fear that the situation was slipping out of his control and that the queen was about to betray him, abandoning him to his fate in Ireland, or that she suspected that he might prove a traitor, fed his anger and led him to a new and unexpected—better, unscripted—move.

Essex returned to England from Ireland at top speed and, still dusty and sweaty from the long voyage, hurried to the royal palace. Without bothering to be announced, he burst through the door to the queen's bedchamber. Elizabeth was in her dressing gown, wigless, and without makeup, an elderly woman surprised in her most intimate setting, her private sphere, in a zone and at a time inaccessible even to her lover—or particularly to her lover. She was taken by surprise, without warning, in her most personal backstage area, with neither the mask of royalty nor the mask of seduction, deprived of both the trappings of the queen and the garments of a woman who wants to appear beautiful and seductive.

With his irruption into her chamber, Essex destroyed both the image of a powerful queen and a seductive woman and of the performance that they had both worked to construct. Deceit and artifice were shattered. Essex had betrayed yet another pact: the fiction linking the young earl and the old queen. He had suddenly switched the script and even the play. Before Elizabeth's own eyes, he betrayed her image of herself as a fascinating woman and as a queen who demands the greatest respect. Essex had betrayed the woman and the queen; he had betrayed the joint performance of Elizabeth and of Essex as accomplices in reciprocal illusion. Essex betrayed the role game, shattered rituals, and with one blow obliterated Elizabeth's sacredness as both woman and queen. Moreover, by actively pursuing the new role that the queen had constructed for him, he confirmed her suspicions. Essex was henceforth an out-and-out traitor. All order had been turned upside down.

How could anyone trust such a man? Could the queen ever believe that breaking so many rules and such great impetuosity had been dictated uniquely by passion, by his eagerness to speak with her and explain himself? Could she think that the strength of his emotions was the sole source of a flooding out of this sort?

Essex's new infraction of the rules brought back instead a memory that still burned within her: Essex, furious and reaching for his sword. His breaking into her private chamber was a betrayal and proof that further betrayals might follow; it confirmed a break that by that time was irreparable; it signaled the definitive dissolution of the We and of the rules that had reinforced the We.

Wounded and betrayed, Elizabeth could only display herself in all her power, send Essex away, and treat him as a traitor. She was forced to betray him in turn: "Elizabeth's anger had assumed a grimmer aspect than ever before. Was this still a lovers' quarrel? If so, it was indeed a strange one. For now contempt, fear, and hatred had come to drop their venom into the deadly brew of disappointed passion. With fixed resentment, as the long months dragged on, she nursed her wrath; she would make him suffer for his incompetence, his insolence, his disobedience; did he imagine that his charms were irresistible? She had had enough of them, and he would find that he had made a mistake."[15]

Essex's only choice was to play the traitor—this time whole-heartedly—and do what Elizabeth expected of him and had always feared. This time the earl was not to disappoint the queen, and he behaved exactly as Elizabeth had foreseen and imagined, as in the best self-fulfilling prophecies.

First Essex betrayed the woman and the formerly adored lover by saying terrible things about her: "On one occasion something was said in his presence of 'Her Majesty's conditions.' 'Her conditions!' he exclaimed. 'Her conditions are as crooked as her carcase!' The intolerable words reached Elizabeth and she never recovered from them."[16]

The earl did not stop at words, however, but passed into action, organizing a plot against the queen. Ambiguity and ambivalence had led to all-out war, with no blows spared on either side. The We that no longer existed abandoned the field to two individuals struggling for power over each other. Essex, treated as a traitor, became one; unleashing his rage and his pride, he used his prestige to attempt to remove Elizabeth from the throne.

He marched on London in a foolish and useless attempt to raise the City against Elizabeth, but the plan failed and he was imprisoned and condemned to death. The queen could still have intervened to spare him, or she could have saved face by leaving him locked up forever in the Tower of London. But his offense to her as a woman and his betrayal of the We, signaled by his irruption into her private chamber and his remark about her crooked carcass, could not be rubbed out: these determined her acts more than his high treason in attempting to strip her of her power. Rather than removing her from the throne, Essex had dropped her from the joint performance that, despite the ups and downs of their relationship, the queen and the earl had staged for their mutual enjoyment. In her own eyes, Elizabeth, now sixty-seven, was a "carcase": the fiction, the performance, had ended. Both had betrayed the script that they themselves had written; both had abandoned the We.

What counted now was to reestablish order by operating within the new framework of betrayal. Essex did not deny his treasonous acts and was imprisoned. For her part, Elizabeth returned to her role as queen, condemning to death the traitor whom she had so dearly loved but who had caused her so much pain. Condemning Essex to death may perhaps have been the last paradoxical gesture of love that Elizabeth could offer him: to be betrayed and suffer the extreme consequences of that betrayal was precisely what Essex expected of her.

Hadn't Essex gone about proclaiming publicly that the queen had abandoned and betrayed him? This time she would not disappoint him. His condemnation to death was also a necessary compensation that Elizabeth had to offer to her own betrayed self. Elizabeth needed to forget her own contribution to the betrayal and redefine herself by attributing all the blame to Essex and punishing him.

There was no other solution to so many reciprocal and interwoven betrayals but to put an end to all interaction and to the relationship itself. One of the two actors had to quit the stage forever. That decision remained in the hands of the person who wielded the most power, which was the queen. Elizabeth and Essex had betrayed each other, increasingly and reciprocally, and each had been the victim of the other's betrayal. Each one's betrayals were interwoven with those of the other, not as an automatic response or a defensive gesture, but rather because of the incessant making and unmaking of interaction that goes back and forth from one individual to the other, that destroys and rebuilds itself continuously, but always creates new interactions and new subjects. When Elizabeth and Essex discovered within themselves that betrayal was a possible part of their interaction, rather than carefully avoiding it, concealing it, or ignoring it, they gave it a voice and room to expand. Both chose to be faithful to betrayal as a new way for them to be themselves and stubbornly defend their own individuality; but at the same time they chose to continue to be present in the relationship. Elizabeth did not react at Essex's first betrayal: she *acted.* Disturbed, she was forced to look at herself, at him, and at their partnership in a new way, which means that she was forced to redefine herself and her relationship with the earl. For his part, Essex did not betray in response to a betrayal, but rather as a way to construct a new role for himself, a new autonomous self, independent of the queen. But even this new self came to light thanks to his relationship with Elizabeth, changed though it was.

The death of Essex and the unhappy ending to the tale was the result of changes that they had brought about in each other and in their relationship, just as the happy encounters of yesteryear had been.

Both parties had always displayed suspicion and trust, comprehension and misunderstandings, support and abandonment, all of which changed over the course of time. Ambivalent accomplices, at one moment participants in a We and at another both strenuously defending their own individuality, Elizabeth and Essex put on a highly tragic performance of betrayal.

4

Secrets and Betrayals

I have more than once been deceived by the person I loved most and of whose love, above everyone else's, I have been most confident; and because of this I have sometimes thought to myself that it may be as well never to trust anyone in this world nor to give oneself as a hostage to a friend, however dear and cherished he may be, to the extent of telling him all one's thoughts without reserve as if he were one's very self. For there are so many concealed places and recesses in our minds that it is humanly impossible to discover and judge the pretenses hidden there.

«BALDASSARE CASTIGLIONE, *The Book of the Courtier*»

Revealing a Secret

Sharing a secret is one way to reinforce and create intimacy. All who share a secret feel themselves part of a privileged and special relationship that excludes those not in the know. Including, but at the same time excluding, is the mark of the secret's ambivalence, often transforming it into an instrument of power. Around the secret—precisely thanks to this dual character—betrayal always lies in wait. Anyone who knows of the existence of a secret and knows that he is excluded from it will be tempted to gain access to it, thus inviting betrayal. On the other hand, the custodians of the secret can betray it by using it as an instrument of power to exclude or include others.

Secrecy creates intimacy and sharing, but also the possibility of betrayal: sharing a secret is a choice that involves the risk of its betrayal. The pleasure of sharing a secret can lead to incautiously testing the risk contained in that sharing. The pleasure of revealing it (a pleasure connected with power), thus enlarging the circle of sharing, can overcome the indecision induced by the idea of betrayal. This may be why revealing a secret is perhaps one of the most widespread forms of betrayal. There are secrets and secrets, but, beyond their content, revealing them is always an act of betrayal.

One can betray secrets tied to explicit pacts, such as those established among friends, confidants, militants in the same political or religious faction, among members of the same family, or between spouses. One can also betray secrets based on an implicit pact, taken for granted and never expressed, such as those of an interpersonal intimacy.

Explicit pacts of secrecy are often reinforced by ritualistic linguistic forms: promises, oaths, or rites of initiation. Someone can confide a secret to a friend and ask him or her to promise not to reveal it, trusting in that informal promise. Here respecting secrecy depends on the affective relationship between the friends rather than on the type of obligation. Entry into a group may involve a formal promise not to reveal its internal secrets, and any failure to respect that obligation will be met with sanctions and punishments. More or less formalized rites surround every secret, however. Naturally, such rites differ according to their context, but their content and symbolic significance are similar. A company or institution demands loyalty and discretion from its employees without requiring a blood pact, whereas membership in a religious or political group or a secret society may involve genuine initiation rites to reinforce the bond of secrecy.

Failure to respect such obligations, by diffusing to the outside world what should remain inaccessible, is a form of betrayal that puts the perpetrator immediately outside of the We. Revealing a family secret, a friend's secret, or a secret of the membership group is both symbolically and concretely a gesture of rupture, a renunciation of the tie that binds, of established pacts, and of the relationship itself. Revealing a secret discredits it as a secret; it devalues it by demoting it from something held sacred to something so ordinary that it can be made public knowledge. Moreover, the devaluation and desacralization of an occurrence or a bit of information supposed to remain secret brings a similar devaluation of the person or persons who had decreed them to be secret. All who have been betrayed in this way react with anger and pain, not only because their trust was betrayed but because something they thought important has been cheapened. They are panic stricken and seized by a feeling of being misunderstood because they find themselves suddenly alone. The differing attitudes toward the importance of keeping a secret by the person who betrays and the person or persons betrayed deals a blow to the relationship. Only the one who imparts a secret knows its full importance. The one who receives it has to accept its worth along with the secret itself, even if the value attributed to it seems to him exaggerated, misplaced, or downright ridiculous. Very often a secret is revealed because the person revealing it considers it less important than did the person who entrusted him with it.

Thus the betrayal of a secret also implies a perception and evaluation gap in the minds of both the one who betrays it and the one who had confided it. Revealing a secret not only shatters secrecy but introduces dissonance into a relationship.

Many relationships are based on sharing a secret: the relationship's reason for being is based on the existence of the secret and the sharers' sense of complicity. This helps us to understand why, although revealing secrets is such a widespread phenomenon, it is seen as one of the most intolerable forms of betrayal.

What interactional processes lead to the betrayal of a pact of secrecy? We can swear, in good faith, to keep a secret that seems important to us at a given moment but later betray it because we have come to see it as ridiculous or irrelevant. Or perhaps we lose interest in the person or group to which we have sworn secrecy; hence, we claim the right not only to change our opinion but to reveal the secret. Or else revealing a secret can be an expression of our detachment, rage, or desire for revenge. In all of these possible explanations, it is not necessarily the one who entrusted the secret who was in error; rather, the processual character of the developing relationship has changed the perceived relevance of the secret or the pact of secrecy. Something that previously had been caged can now be allowed to fly free. Another possibility is that someone might decide, unilaterally, that although the secret and the relationship that preserved it are still sacred, it can be shared with others. When this happens, the person who reveals the secret does not view sharing it as betrayal, but simply as transmission of the secret to others who will respect it and who can be asked for promises, oaths, and reassurances of secrecy. This produces an open secret—what is known in Italian as a "secret of Pulcinella"—that everyone knows of but pretends not to know. To betray a secret by transmitting it to others—that is, by including others in the group that keeps the secret—often happens when someone belongs to more than one social circle and has a number of opportunities for encounters and relations with people he thinks will keep the secret. This form of transfer of a secret often brings no advantage to the person who betrays it aside from seeming to be "in the know" and enjoying the pleasure of deciding who will be admitted into an exclusive relationship.

Other people's secrets can also be betrayed for material rewards, as is the case with military, industrial, and professional secrets that can be sold to the highest bidder. On occasion this sort of betrayal is repaid by admission to or affiliation with an opposing group that is hostile to or in rivalry with the group that was the source of the secret.

Moving from one social circle to another, one group to another, or even one relationship to another can require (explicitly or implicitly) the revelation of a secret as a sign of membership in the new group. Relations of friendship, and love relationships in particular, seem to set a high price on this sort of proof. Entry into the relationship demands the betrayal of old forms of membership through the revelation of their secrets, paradoxically offering proof of one's loyalty and participation in the new relationship by means of a betrayal. Relationships based on a demand for total and radical openness, impossible as that goal may be, tolerate no secrets. Parties to such relationships feel they have to know everything about the other person or persons, denying all possibility that they might have secrets with outsiders. Thus it can happen that in order to prove one's own dedication to and trust in a friend, a lover, or a spouse, other people's secrets have to be immolated on the altar of the new relationship.

It can happen that secrets about others will be revealed in order to shift attention from those we hold dear. We draw attention away from what we really want to keep hidden by revealing someone else's secret, in legitimate defense of our own. By displaying our generosity at others' expense, we gain more than one advantage. When we reveal a secret, we seem to be part of intriguing and mysterious relations and uncommon relationships and events. We make others feel good because they are privileged to have been chosen as the recipient of our secrets. We use betrayal as a form of seduction of a new person or group that we want to conquer.

Within intimate relations, the bed is the sociological space in which this sort of betrayal takes place most frequently. This is true whether it is the matrimonial bed, a bed shared with a lover, or a bed on which adolescents or female friends can sit for hours chatting and exchanging confidences sworn to secrecy.

Precisely because the marriage bed is a highly symbolic and ritualized place, it becomes a sort of confessional where spouses recite their roles of reciprocal fidelity and strengthen the tie that binds by telling everybody else's secrets, in the process betraying friends, relatives, colleagues, and at times even lovers. Moreover, the more marriage shifts from being an institutional or passionate relationship to a relationship of friendship between equals—what Anthony Giddens calls "a pure relationship"—the more other people's secrets tend to be betrayed.[1]

In his novel *A Heart So White*, Javier Marías states that marriage is a narrative institution:

For the sake of love or its essence—telling, informing, announcing, commenting, opining, distracting, listening and laughing, and vainly making plans—one betrays everyone else, friends, parents, brothers and sisters, blood relations and non-blood relations, former lovers and beliefs, former mistresses, your own past and childhood, your own language when you stop speaking it and doubtless your country, everything that anyone holds to be secret or perhaps merely belongs to the past. In order to flatter the person you love you denigrate everything else in existence, you deny and abominate everything in order to content and reassure the one person who could leave you.[2]

Similarly, as we shall soon see, Emma, the protagonist of Harold Pinter's *Betrayal*, shares more secrets with her husband than with her lover; she confesses her adultery with Jerry to her husband, but she never tells Jerry that her husband knows everything.[3]

The Secrets of Intimacy

There are betrayals of secrecy that are perceived as such even when they do not involve oaths or promises. I am referring to the revelation of the innocent minor secrets of everyday life and of the sphere of privacy and intimacy, to which only participants or authorized spectators are admitted. These include how much time it takes us to get dressed, what ritual reassurances we need before we can go to sleep or leave the house, what we fear, our obsessions or idiosyncrasies, what nicknames we give our partner, and so forth. These are things that the self holds sacred and that we do not divulge indiscriminately. Precisely because we hold everything that belongs to our private sphere to be sacred and impregnable, we take it for granted that anyone who is admitted to it will refrain from speaking about it with others and will respect it with their silence. This might be a form of what Goffman calls "tactful inattention."[4]

There is no need to ask for oaths or extract promises from those who are admitted into the private sphere of our everyday life, because we trust them. Rather than genuine secrets, what we share with them is indistinct areas of secrecy within which what counts is not the gesture, the act, or the word, but the secret's symbolic significance. We feel ourselves betrayed if someone—a family member, a good friend, a partner, a spouse, or a colleague—with whom we feel secure because we share a space in which we can exhibit our neuroses or our tics turns the spotlight onto our offstage personalities by revealing our behaviors or words to others. Goffman calls it betrayal when a member of a team—a group of friends, a professional group, or even a casual acquaintance—publicly reveals particulars of the team's "backstage" life.[5]

These betrayals and revelations of intimacy are quite common, and they are genuine attacks on relations and interactions because they sanction a break in complicity, a retreat, even if a momentary one, from the We. Anyone who betrays in this manner willingly moves away from the collective representation, allies himself or herself with the others, passes over to the side of the audience, thus betraying (in the etymological sense of *trādere*) by transferring from one side to the other fragments of our life that are insignificant only in appearance.

The person so betrayed finds himself removed from his proper place, alone and nude on the stage, exposed to the gaze of others with no time to put on his social mask. The betrayal is experienced as an abandonment (because it *is* an abandonment, even if only a temporary one, and a declaration of separation), but also as an attack on the person's most intimate sphere.

Sharing the secrecy of intimacy reinforces unity and connection; its betrayal signals a rupture that can be irreparable. For example, young people facing puberty and adolescence feel betrayed when their parents reveal their anxieties and fears or details of their private lives to adult friends or any member of the adult community. The young feel themselves defrauded and their trust unappreciated. They may ask their parents not to talk about them and make a point of not confiding in them in the future. It is not what is revealed that is important here but rather the very fact that something was revealed—that implicit pacts of complicity and sharing were not respected.

Many young girls tell of feeling betrayed and abandoned when their mother proudly reveals to friends that the daughter has begun to menstruate. What was supposed to have remained protected within the sphere of intimacy and complicity of the mother-daughter relationship is suddenly unveiled before the eyes of the world. In this case the mother betrays the daughter's trust and denies her right to privacy. Not only does the mother's betrayal suddenly shift her to the opposing side and ally her with the general public; it shows that she fails to recognize the relationship and, by denying her daughter's privacy, disavows her as a person. The mother betrays by violating the rules of discretion, which Simmel declares to be "nothing but the feeling that there exists a right in regard to the sphere of the immediate life contents."[6]

This subtle but nonetheless painful form of betrayal always lies in wait for us because we are all ambivalent toward others. We want both a sense of belonging to a group and distance from it—both complicity and estrangement, involvement and detachment, protection and emancipation. Thus we all need to assert our autonomy from time to time. What better way to do so than through a public display of autonomy in a demonstrative and highly meaningful act that puts estrangement and separateness at center stage? And what act is more significant symbolically than betrayal?

To quit an intimacy by betraying it is one way to reassert one's own individuality; it is a declaration of nonmembership. As such, it also signals an invitation to the other to contemplate our own irreducible alterity: "I am not We"; "I am not You"; "I am moving off, passing from one side to the other; I cannot be imprisoned in any relationship."

This assertion of alterity and nonaffiliation seems to be what is concealed behind the betrayal of intimacy and of the private sphere. It is probable that by revealing particulars of intimacy and stripping a shared experience of its sacredness by telling others about it that we express a desire to move on, to take part in other secrecies, conquer new spaces for interaction, establish new complicities, or add new ones to the usual ones. By revealing the secret area of our life in common with another, we declare our own independence and our own complicity with whomever or whatever functions as a public, an audience, thus signaling that we are available for new intimacies. Whether this occurs consciously or unconsciously matters little: the fact remains that the secret revealed becomes, even in this case, a reckoning, a symbolic bill to pay.

And yet we all continue to trust in discretion and secrecy, because otherwise any form of social life would be impossible. In order to enter into relations with others we need to feel sure that they will not violate the invisible but impenetrable boundaries that we all choose to place around ourselves. Life in society is made possible thanks to the fact that, on the one hand, we all know that others can be shown only what we think opportune, and that, on the other hand, in return our own secrecy and privacy will be respected. Should it happen (as it has in some totalitarian regimes) that persons or institutions try to violate privacy or demand absolute transparency, individuals tend to reconstruct their own zones of inviolability, shifting the boundaries of those zones and taking greater care to conceal zones that have not yet been invaded. Violation of the secrets of privacy thus leads to even greater secrecy in defense of individuality and of our ability to enter into relations with others. If we were sure that we could keep no secrets, we would not enter into any form of life in society.

What criteria can we use to define what is sacred and secret within the sphere of intimacy? The subjects participating in any particular interaction define it and establish its explicit and implicit rules. Every interaction and every relationship that involves the intimate and private sphere is subject to ongoing definition of what is and is not to be kept secret. Social definitions of the sphere of intimacy enter in to these free definitions as well, however. What is considered private and secret is determined not only by the will of the individuals involved but also by how the private sphere is constructed socially and then interiorized by those individuals. Socially permitted revelations of intimacy also depend on the relevance and social significance that a particular historical and social context gives to the intimate sphere.

At the court of Versailles, for example, the sovereign's most intimate and personal acts—getting dressed and undressed, waking up and going to bed—were public events to which the nobility was admitted, precisely because the very idea of privacy did not exist and individual secret zones were kept strictly internal.

The betrayal of intimacy, understood as the revelation of gestures, actions, and behaviors in private life, is a form of betrayal that takes on relevance and dramatic impact only with the constitution of a separate sphere of intimacy and privacy.[7] Individuality had to be declared sacred and the right to privacy had to be affirmed before indiscretion and the revelation of intimacy could be viewed as betrayal. Simmel claims that only with the modern age did a right to private property, material and spiritual, come into being: "Just as material property is, so to speak, an extension of the ego, and any interference with our property is, for this reason, felt to be a violation of the person, there also is an intellectual private property, whose violation effects a lesion of the ego in its very center."[8] The affirmation of a right to individual private property led to demands for the right to inviolable physical spaces (zones of the house such as the bedroom carefully hidden from outsiders), along with a right to defend portions of the self held to be exclusively intimate and private. Discretion, a quality that had always been necessary to the flow of social relations and to sociability (we need only recall how Monsignor Della Casa's *Galateo* or Baldassare Castiglione's *Book of the Courtier* continually stress rules of discretion), became a right in the modern age. The right to privacy and the right to discretion were established simultaneously.

In this sense, betrayal of intimacy is a modern form of betrayal; it accompanies not only a sacralization of the private sphere but also the formation of modern individuality, which is increasingly aware of its own jealously guarded boundaries and is increasingly suspended between membership and detachment. The modern subject defends intimacy in two ways. On the one hand, the intimate sphere is protected from the indiscreet gaze of nonparticipants thanks to laws and procedures to safeguard privacy and to the construction of spaces and times inaccessible to outsiders.

On the other hand, however, modern individuals fear that excessive intimacy might overwhelm their individuality even within the sanctified circle of privacy; thus, they tend to withdraw even further and construct a personal privacy within the well-defended confines of the private sphere.

The modern individual desperately seeks a time and a space that cannot be shared with anyone else, continually repositioning the boundaries of personal inviolability, using ever-new secrecies as defense and protection. Thus secrets multiply indefinitely. A secret zone of unique and exclusive individuality to which only a few members of the private circle are given entry is added to the secret sphere of private life not open to outsiders, which includes family relationships, friendships, and loves. An ultimate secret zone is shared with no one and excludes everyone else. While we all establish a private world that we may share with freely chosen others, we also claim the right to escape from always being "a part of" something external thanks to an exclusive and purely individual privacy.

A betrayal of intimacy can lurk in this contradictory affirmation and negation of private life, this oscillation between a defense of being together with others we have chosen and a defense against those same others, and between a desire to be with others and the desire to be only for ourselves. The same individual who feels wounded and abandoned when his or her intimate sphere is revealed is quick to betray the intimacy of others if that is what it takes to assert personal autonomy. That individual is both betrayer and betrayed, at one moment participating in a group and at another playing the solitary knight errant—alternately high priest of the sacredness of the private sphere and desecrating rebel.

Concealing a Secret

Jealously keeping a secret to oneself without sharing it with those who are closest can also be considered a betrayal of trust. Within a relationship, concealing portions of oneself and one's life can come to be perceived as a form of withdrawal, a sign of mistrust and evidence of duplicity. To discover a hidden secret is to discover the other's lack of transparency, the ambiguity that is an integral part of both the individual and every form of interaction. As Simmel puts it: "We are, after all, made in such a way that we need not only a certain proportion of truth and error as the basis of our lives . . . but also a certain proportion of distinctness and indistinctness in the image of our life-elements."[9]

Whenever we discover that the other has a secret, we feel betrayed. Tolerating the other's secrecy, being willing not to discover secrets, accepting their multiplicity without feeling betrayed is an art difficult to acquire and to practice. What is more likely to happen, especially in intimate relationships (friendships, love relationships, family relations), is that we demand to know everything about the other and feel offended and betrayed when we find that a secret has been kept from us.

All forms of interaction are based on trust: we have to trust the image that the other projects and trust that he or she will do his or her part in the interaction. That trust is not limited to the *hic et nunc*, however: we trust the other not only when he or she stands before us, in the interaction of the moment, but also over time. This is what enables us to enjoy and to speak of a lasting interaction.

The extension of trust over time produces a number of expectations. We expect that the other, even in our absence, will remain true to the image that he or she has shown to us and will reveal his or her entire self when we are together. This expectation of loyalty protracted through time is more strongly felt in relationships that involve sentiments, emotions, and intimacy, particularly in relations of friendship and love. Even if we know that the other is involved in multiple relationships, treads many stages, and plays many roles, we tend to retain a homogeneous and coherent image of him or her. Moreover, we perform before the other as if before a privileged audience, a public ready to accept all sorts of performances and that we can permit to see both the spectacle taking place on stage and what goes on backstage.

We presuppose that the other has no secrets from us, forgetting that what two parties to an interaction know about the other "is interwoven with elements known to only one of the two."[10]

We all know that we have secrets from one another, but we presuppose that the other has no secrets: we feel ourselves betrayed every time we discover secrets, hidden facets, other selves. Still, there is a shadowy zone in every relationship and every interaction: Marías tells us that we believe that we know those close to us, but time bears with it many more unknown things than familiar things, and we know proportionally less and less. There are always more shadowy zones.[11]

Precisely because all individuals involved in intimate relationships feel the pressure of the other's expectations that he or she will know all, they desperately seek to keep intact and inviolate the ideal sphere of secrecy that is the self. Betrayal thus arises from a tension between the other's expectations and a defense of the self; between the narrative requirements of interaction (the claim that everything must be told) and of secrecy (where each party tries to defend his or her own ideal sphere).

Betrayal is perceived as such either because we feel that the other did not trust us fully, thus betraying the pact to share and trust implicit in every relationship, or because we discover that the other is leading "another life" and possesses another self from which we are excluded. The real extent of the secret—whether it relates to minor details or more important events and thoughts—hardly matters: we feel ourselves betrayed by the very fact that the other has withdrawn from total sharing by keeping something hidden. Naturally, this type of betrayal is perceived differently according to circumstance: the more pervasive the relations or the stronger the pact of mutual and absolute openness, the more the subjects feel themselves betrayed.

Even if we claim that we want to know everything about the other, however, we are well aware of our own need to withdraw, to hide ourselves, to keep secrets, in order to maintain the relationship. Although we want to know everything about the other and we feel ourselves betrayed when we run into closed doors that conceal secrets, we are betrayers because we cannot survive without setting aside and hiding some parts of ourselves—events and experiences that we defend, considering them our exclusive province. Simmel states, "Intimate relations, whose formed medium is physical and psychological nearness, lose the attractiveness, even the content of their intimacy, as soon as the close relationship does not also contain, simultaneously and alternatingly, distances and intermissions."[12]

Interaction is possible as long as the dividing line between the I and the You, between what is me and what is other than me, remains distinct. If that border is threatened or besieged by demands for fusion or radical honesty, the interaction itself is in danger. The distinction between the I and the You, between two different individualities, presupposes that each of us contains areas that the other cannot know. When these hidden zones are violated by excessive indiscretion, we tend to reconstruct them anew, to move our secrets elsewhere in legitimate defense of our individuality. Individuality is a plant that thrives best in an intermediate zone between light and shadow, and that will ineluctably perish if exposed to too much sunlight.

Secrecy, concealment from the other, becomes an integral and fundamental part of intersubjectivity, which, as Simmel states, requires an incommensurably changing measure of reciprocal secrecy: "Relationships . . . presuppose a certain ignorance and a measure of mutual concealment, even though this measure varies immensely, to be sure." Intersubjectivity exists precisely because individualities in need of protection exist: "An ideal sphere lies around every human being. Although differing in size in various directions and differing according to the person with whom one entertains relations, this sphere cannot be penetrated, unless the personality value of the individual is thereby destroyed."[13]

The fact that the ideal sphere that forms and protects individuality is not constructed once and for all, but rather changes, growing or shrinking according to the intersubjective context, makes total knowledge of the other even more impossible. With each occasion that arises, individuals choose the form and importance to give to the ideal sphere depending on the interaction and who is involved. We know about everyone else what they want us to know; we show to everyone else only what we want them to know. To be an individual is above all to have the freedom to choose one's own secrecy; it is the freedom to have inviolable boundaries.

Many marriages fail precisely because of a lack of secrecy and mutual discretion, when habit takes over and there is no longer any surprise. On the other hand, the sense that behind every revelation—every moment of openness, even when honesty seems absolute—there lies something secret, something still to be discovered, leads the partners to mutual conquest and seduction, day after day. This sort of ongoing surprise is the reward for self-control, even within the most intimate relationship, concerning the inner private property of the other. Here the right to secrecy limits the right to ask questions.

In *The Key*, a novel by Junichiro Tanizaki, a middle-aged couple rekindles the eroticism and passion of their conjugal relationship through the introduction of secrets and secrecy.[14] The husband is keeping a diary, in which he confides his lack of sexual satisfaction and all that he cannot say openly to his wife without violating discretion and modesty. Even though he entrusts his most secret thoughts to the written page, he is so sure that his wife will not read them that he decides to leave the key to the drawer in which he keeps the diary out in plain view. What matters is that the wife knows he is keeping a secret, not that she knows what it is. This sets off a game of hide and seek that is not only highly erotic but also arouses enormous curiosity in both husband and wife about the secret—or, better, about the existence of something secret. Neither considers the content of the secret of any great importance; what matters is that each knows that the other has a secret. The husband confesses to his diary, "Secretly, I may have accepted, even hoped, that she was reading it. Then why do I lock the drawer and hide the key? Besides, if I leave it where she is likely to see it, she may think: 'This was written for my benefit.'. . . She may even think: 'His real diary is somewhere else.'"[15]

The game consists in stimulating the other's curiosity, in rousing the suspicion that there is always another secret, that a violated secrecy reconstitutes its virginity elsewhere. The husband wants his secret to be discovered, but he wants the discovery of the diary to happen secretly and without ever being admitted to. It is as if there were a permanent free zone, continually reconstructed, the existence of which the other knows, but without knowing its exact location. What is important is that each knows that the other has a diary and is capable of having secrets. The entire story that Tanizaki narrates in alternating diary entries depends on an existential and erotic need for self-affirmation through secrecy. The accent is not on the content of their secrets but rather on the fact that each recognizes that the other is secretive, is concealing something and rejecting an illusory transparency.

The wife begins to keep a diary. "One reason why keeping a diary appeals to me," she writes, "is that although I know exactly where to find his, he won't even realize I have one. That gives me a delicious sense of superiority."[16] The husband soon discovers his wife's diary, however, and they both begin to read the other's entries, still pretending to be unaware of the existence of the other's diary. "Now that it is obviously being read by someone else," the wife writes after realizing that her husband is reading her diary, "I suppose I ought to abandon it. Yet the 'someone' is my own husband, and we have an unspoken agreement to behave as if we weren't aware of each other's secrets."[17]

When the husband discovers his wife's diary, what he fears above all is the loss of secrecy. He expresses the hope that his wife, knowing that her secret has been discovered, will never write the truth, but instead will secretly maintain secrecy. He mentions a family friend with whom she may or may not have been flirting and writes, "Ikuko, I beg of you, don't confess! Even though I'll not see it, don't make such a confession! Lie if you must."[18]

Secrecy thus becomes a model for their affective relationship, rekindling their love and raising the possibility of other loves. It permits both the husband and the wife to express their full

sexuality as their sexual relations become more and more satis-
fying and their eroticism increasingly enhanced. Even their cou-
pling takes place secretly, in a staging of secrecy. He caresses her,
looks at her, and possesses her only when she is asleep, and she,
feigning sleep, enjoys sexual relations as never before. Only by
being restored to themselves, fleeing all fusion, can each of them
recapture personal pleasure and give pleasure to the other. At the
same time, each one achieves a sense of self thanks to pretense
and to a withdrawal from a pervasive relationship. What is not
said—the secrecy—thus becomes not only a source of pleasure
but the basis for a relational intensity and a mutual comprehension that they never could have realized through absolute
transparency or openness.

Choosing to keep portions of the self secret, and managing to
keep them secret, is an affirmation of autonomy, a way to withdraw from the fixed gaze of the other. As we grow up and become
adults, we learn to distinguish between the "I" and the world, to
construct filters for selective communication, and to withdraw
when we so desire. Learning to keep our thoughts and fantasies
secret, learning to distinguish not only between what we can and
cannot say but above all between what we want and do not want
to say, is part of the process of individuation. We get to know, and
to know how to operate within, a second world that lies beside
the manifest world.

When we discover that we can hide things, including ourselves, thus making it impossible for the other to know everything about us, we also learn that absolute knowledge of the other
is impossible. By discovering that we can withdraw from the pervasive gaze of the other or others and live in a secret world, we
realize that we can be free, but also that we can deceive and
betray, at least by our silence.

But if there are things others cannot know about me, there are
also things that I cannot know about them. Similarly, if I can deceive and betray, so can the other. To conceal a secret involves
the art of dissimulation, which is not only the ability to deceive
the other but also the ability to defend our own freedom and

autonomy. To dissimulate, to keep secrets, and not to reveal everything about ourselves is thus a way to escape from the power of the pervasive gaze of the other. As Michel Foucault suggests, it is a form of resistance to a power that seeks to colonize not only external behaviors but also consciousness. Following Foucault, Remo Bodei writes:

> The practice of dissimulation produces unexpected positive effects; in fact, it increases the sagacity and the introspective capacities of the individual, rendering him more familiar with himself, with his own ideas and motivations; it accentuates detachment from the temporal immediacy of lived experiences and doubles the I object with another I who is the subject of the observation, thus facilitating self-control and sovereignty over one's own affect.[19]

Secrecy is a form of relation and communication that makes these two things possible by marking a distinction between them but, at the same time, it threatens them because is makes withdrawal, deceit, and betrayal possible.

Often what is kept hidden has no relevance to the interaction, and it may even be extremely banal and insignificant. But the less important it is, the more we feel ourselves betrayed, because the only explanation that we manage to find is the most painful one: the other is marking his distance from us; he or she is hiding, withdrawing.

Harold Pinter's play *Betrayal* offers an extraordinary example of chain-reaction betrayal for the purpose of flight and withdrawal. Emma, who is married to Robert, betrays him with Jerry, a mutual friend, but Emma also betrays Jerry by lying to him and hiding from him not only important facts but insignificant details. Emma has never revealed to Jerry that Robert knows about their relationship, which has been going on for a good five years. This means that she is hiding an important fact from him. But she also lies to him continually about small details of her daily life, either by changing them or concealing them.

Robert in turn betrays Emma with many other women, and he betrays his friend Jerry by never revealing to him, although the two see each other often, that he knows about Jerry's relations with his wife. When Jerry discovers that Robert has always known everything, he feels betrayed by both his friend and by Emma. He discovers that, during five years of love and friendship, much has been concealed from him and that the two people who are the closest to him have a secret life from which they have excluded him:

> What a funny thing. We were such close friends, weren't we, Robert and me, even though I haven't seen him for a few months, but through all those years, all the drinks, all the lunches... we had together, I never even gleaned... I never suspected... that there was anyone else... in his life but you. Never. For example, when you're with a fellow in a pub, or a restaurant, for example, from time to time he pops out for a piss, you see, who doesn't, but what I mean is, if he's making a crafty telephone call, you can sort of sense it, you see, you can sense the pip pip pips. Well, I never did that with Robert. He never made any pip pip telephone calls in any pub I was ever with him in. The funny thing is that it was me who made the pip pip calls—to you, when I left him boozing at the bar. That's the funny thing.[20]

Jerry feels his friendship betrayed because Robert has shown him only a part of himself. But when he reproaches Robert for having kept silent about his adventures and having always known about his relations with Emma, Robert justifies his actions, proclaiming his own version of loyalty: although he continues to enjoy meeting his wife's lovers, he stops playing squash with them.

Thus Robert has sent Jerry a clear signal. By no longer playing squash with him, Robert redefines their friendship and reduces the space of their interactions. Not playing squash together means shutting down an exclusively male symbolic space in which friends talk about everything from women to sports. Jerry should have known that Robert's withdrawal from that symbolic space should be interpreted as a signal of a change within their friendship.

In the course of this novel, everyone betrays everyone else, and everyone withdraws, concealing parts of himself or herself from the other. The boundaries of what each knows about the other become increasingly unclear. What is left unsaid becomes both the presupposition for and the form of these complex and ambivalent interactions. What the other knows or does not know is completely uncertain, and there are no principles or criteria to define what should be said and what should be hidden. Each character remains alone and wants to remain alone, fleeing every excessively demanding relationship. The fear of losing one's self with the other and in the other pushes them all to accumulate deceits and betrayals as the only way to withdraw and seek their own selves.

The five years of the relations between Emma and Jerry are not only five years of adultery but the time span and the place of a reciprocal withdrawal. Emma conceals many more secrets from her lover than from her husband: in this tale, the one who knows least is the lover, which means that he is doubly betrayed.

The interaction between the lovers, Emma and Jerry, demands a dose of secrecy, a necessary withdrawal. If in fact telling everything to one another is particular to the interaction between husband and wife, to the point of becoming "a narrative institution," many things remain unsaid in the interaction between lovers. Lovers do not tell one another everything: they avoid banality; they cultivate mystery; they behave according to different rules. They speak a different language and dress differently from a married couple. Even their eroticism is played out on a different level, where secrecy plays a fundamental role. In this sense, Emma's concealment, withdrawal, and lying, although they seem to be a betrayal, are instead proof of extreme loyalty to the interaction between lovers and of respect for the rules of that game.

Emma and Robert, on the other hand, precisely because they are husband and wife, tell each other more. Even if they betray one another and withdraw from a reciprocal and total possession of one another, where Jerry is concerned they play at interpreting the role that psychoanalysis calls the hidden observer, the person who knows something the others do not know and who enjoys watching the others while remaining unobserved.[21]

Although Emma and Robert betray one another, they join to-gether to betray Jerry, and they enjoy both their complicity and their reciprocal distance. Thanks to their concealment and with-drawal, Emma, Robert, and Jerry are incapable of telling the same story, and each has a personal version of what happens. The text is full of phrases such as "I thought that you knew" and "Do you really believe that she doesn't know that?"

JERRY: You hadn't thought of telling Judith? [Judith is Jerry's wife]
ROBERT: Telling Judith what? Oh, about you and Emma. You mean to
    say she never knew? Are you quite sure?[22]

Each character's memories fail to agree with the others' mem-ories, even in minor details. The play begins with the contrasting accounts that Emma and Jerry give of their common memories. Times and place are different for Emma and Jerry: each has a per-sonal story to tell, thus denying, even in their memories, that they participated wholly in the relationship. Not only do they elude one another but each cites testimony that definitely denies their joint experience, here, of Jerry tossing Emma's child into the air:

JERRY: Yes, everyone was there that day, standing around, your hus-
    band, my wife, all the kids, I remember.
EMMA: What day?
JERRY: When I threw her up. It was in your kitchen.
EMMA: It was in your kitchen.[23]

The Need for Secrecy

Imprisonment in solitary confinement with the light perpetually on is not only one of the most unbearable tortures, it is also a metaphor for a total violation of secrecy and a determination to shed light on personal dark zones, external and internal. No one can attempt to impose a general and indiscriminate rule of abso-lute sincerity and transparency:

The Soul selects her own Society—
Then—shuts the Door—

To her divine Majority—
Present no more—

Unmoved—she notes the Chariots—pausing—
At her low Gate—
Unmoved—an Emperor be kneeling
Upon her Mat—

I've known her—from an ample nation—
Choose One—
Then—close the Valves of her attention—
Like Stone—

« *Emily Dickinson*, "The Soul selects her own Society" »

Even with that "One" selected from among many, the individual constructs bits of secrecy and ambiguous spaces to avoid fusion or the mutual annihilation of the I and the You. Moments of truth and transparency alternate with moments of secrecy and opacity, truth with error. Clarity and indistinctness play an equal part in interactions.

Although this oscillation between revelation and concealment is the stuff of individuality and intersubjectivity, it can take on a different rhythm and pace according to the relationship and the expectations and desires of the parties involved. What they choose to reveal or keep secret is defined as they go along, following the *hic et nunc* relationship and the way both subjects define the interaction based on their shifting feelings and interests, rational calculations, and emotional urges.

Secrecy can play an infinite number of roles within a relationship, to the point of determining its character. Some relationships are reinforced precisely by an awareness that secrets exist on both sides and through mutual respect of those secrets.

Other relationships, however, are based on pacts of absolute openness and banish the mere thought of even the least secret. Those involved in such relationships are even more exposed to the risk of betrayal. The disclosure of every slight event, fact, or even thought that is not shared produces discomfort, disorientation, and a perception of having been betrayed in terms of the pact of reciprocal honesty and transparency that had been established.

As Frank Pittman demonstrates in his study of adultery, the couples that define themselves as open and tolerant of reciprocal infidelity reach a crisis when one partner learns of an adventure or a relationship that the other has not spoken about.[24] Here the perception of having been betrayed does not derive from the existence of sentimental and sexual relations outside the couple, but rather from the fact that they remained hidden.

The varying degree of secrecy (hence the varying degree of openness) in every relationship depends on how the relationship actually develops, not simply on the intentions of the individuals involved. Highly intimate relationships can be very solid, thanks precisely to a reciprocal concealment of behaviors and actions that would undermine the relationship. Other, less intimate relations, perhaps because they demand less, can tolerate a larger measure of truth:

> "Look," I said, "people who keep secrets for a long time don't always do so out of shame or in order to protect themselves, sometimes it's to protect others, or to preserve a friendship, or a love affair, or a marriage, to make life more tolerable for their children or to shield them from some fear, of which they usually have many. Maybe they simply don't want to add to the world a story they wished had never happened. Not talking about it is like erasing it, forgetting it a little, denying it, not telling a story can be a small favor one does to the world. You have to respect that. You might not want to know everything about me, later on, as time goes by, you might not want to, and I won't want to know everything about you either. You wouldn't want a son of ours to know everything about us. About us when we were separate, for example, before we met. Not even we know everything about each other, neither before, when we were apart nor now, when we're together."[25]

I have chosen to cite this rather long passage from Javier Marías's *A Heart So White* because it seems to me to explain how ambiguity and secrecy can at times become radical forms of loyalty and deliberate choices of fidelity rather than deceitful forms of communication and intersubjectivity. "Not telling a story can be a small favor one does to the world," because the world, which means other people, can tolerate neither an excess of sincerity and transparency nor the whole truth. This means that we can choose to conceal a secret in order to protect both the other and the relationship or to satisfy a tacit request of another who does not necessarily want to know all. Quite often the terminally ill or a betrayed husband or wife send a clear message that they do not want to know the whole truth, and we can prove our loyalty to them only by respecting those desires. Absolute sincerity betrays both the expectations of those who do not want to know and the trust that they have placed in nonverbal communication. If we speak, if we suddenly reveal something, we betray the person who wanted protection. We betray him because we have forced him to know, because we have brusquely destroyed the complex mechanism of self-deceit for which he asked our complicity. Hence betrayal can also lie in revealing something that the other does not want to know. What is unpardonable here is confession, not silence.

This is what happens in Madame de La Fayette's *La princesse de Clèves* when the princess, although she has committed no act of infidelity, admits to her husband that the visit of the Duke of Nemours has troubled her, and she asks her husband to take her away from Paris. This confession, even if it is a proof of fidelity and of her desire to remain faithful, throws her husband into deep distress. The unexpected avowal is "not in the script": it is a highly unusual occurrence between husband and wife and highly inconsonant with the models of behavior of the court, where adultery and flirtation are widespread and tolerated and deceit, intrigues, and lies are just one mode of relationship among many. His wife's absolute sincerity mortally wounds the prince and disorients him to the point that he feels himself doubly betrayed: "You have made me unhappy by the greatest proof of loyalty and trust that any wife ever gave her husband," the Prince of Clèves exclaims.[26] He has suddenly discovered that his wife is capable of passions much more overwhelming than the tranquil affection she has shown him thus far. His wife is thus different from the way he imagined her; instead of the cold woman she has always shown herself to be, she is instead so impassioned that she fears she will be unable to control herself, which is precisely why she asks for his aid. She has another face, another nature that is not only not reserved for him alone, it is hidden from him; she has not committed adultery, but she has been disturbed by emotions he has not thought her capable of. In short, his wife has revealed a secret that she would have done better to have concealed.

With her sincerity, the Princess of Clèves has thrown the normal order of things into disarray: wives do not confess to their husbands that they are teetering on the brink of infidelity. She has upset a relationship based on respect, discretion, secrecy, and reciprocal distance, in which a gesture as impulsive, indiscrete, and violent as confession is unthinkable. The princess has betrayed him by revealing what should have remained hidden.

This is precisely the sort of betrayal that the prince can tolerate least well: his wife has abruptly changed the nature and the rules of their relationship. He is now without a role and has no idea what he should or could do. The role of the husband whose wife reveals her fear of committing an infidelity is new and untested, not only for the Prince of Clèves but for any man of his time. The princess has betrayed him because she has suddenly changed the script; she has left him profoundly embarrassed, unsure of his lines. This is why her admission so upsets the prince that he dies of unhappiness soon after. The only practical thing he can do is to quit the stage.

Keeping a secret, avoiding impulsive narration and unasked-for confession involves renunciation of all aggressive tendencies and all temptation to hasten events by using the power of words. Keeping a secret is also a choice marked by ambivalence, because it is a renunciation of all narcissistic claims to make things happen, calling them into being by naming them, but at the same time it is an equally narcissistic assertion of a desire to be the only one who does or can know.

Hiding portions of the self or the events of one's own life is also a power choice, a wielding of an absolute power that excludes all others. In keeping a secret there is in fact an act of exclusion, an affirmation of wanting to and being able to be self-sufficient, despite the other, despite intimacy. It is an attack that strikes at the heart of the relationship. On the other hand, when a secret is unveiled, even through a betrayal of trust, there is a move to include rather than exclude. Revelation shatters or strikes at the relationship, but its aim is not rejection. It affirms aggressiveness; it is a hostile act, but not a gesture of cancellation.

Naturally, I am not speaking of the greater or lesser morality of one attitude over the other with respect to the possible betrayals that lodge within secrecy; nor am I talking about whether undergoing one form of betrayal is worse than another. What I have sought to analyze is how the very existence of a secret bears within it diverse forms and possibilities of betrayal, and how, paradoxically, an unrevealed secret can be perceived as being just as much a betrayal as a secret revealed.

Thanks to its polysemia, the secret can take on various roles within interactions and relations; it can become a form of communication whether it is concealed or revealed.[27]

Rosencrantz and Guildenstern

In Shakespeare's *Hamlet* the main plot set off by the assassination of the king of Denmark, treacherously killed by his brother, is accompanied by a subplot of the friendship between Rosencrantz and Guildenstern and the young Prince Hamlet. It is a tale of betrayal that turns around secrecy and the ambivalence of relationships.

After the death of his father, Hamlet, pretending to be mad, chooses to conceal his nature and his doubts and thoughts, withdrawing from a reality that seems to him horrible and senseless and constructing a secret world indecipherable to others. As the new king says of him, "Nor th'exterior nor the inward man / Resembles that it was (*Hamlet*, 2.2.6–7; Bevington, 1087).

Keeping this inner world secret becomes for Hamlet the only way to survive physically *and* to keep intact his own interiority and capacity for judgment, so that he can pursue his search for his self and for meaning, a search that, even more than revenge, he has set as his reason for living. Only his friend Horatio is admitted into his secret world, which includes his vision of his father's ghost, his feigned madness, his anxious search for meaning, and his plans for revenge.

It is precisely Hamlet's choice of secrecy and his will to withdraw that generate many betrayals. The king and the queen sense that Hamlet is hiding a secret that makes him elusive, and hence he is suspect and a threat to them. If they are to reestablish their control and their power over the young prince, they must dismantle his defenses and trick him into divulging that secret, cost what it may. In that aim they call to court two old and dear friends of Hamlet's, Rosencrantz and Guildenstern:

> . . . I entreat you both
> That, being of so young days brought up with him,
> And sith so neighbour'd to his youth and havior,
> That you vouchsafe your rest here in our court
> Some little time, so by your companies
> To draw him on to pleasures, and to gather
> So much as from occasion you may glean,
> Whether aught to us unknown afflicts him thus,
> That, open'd, lies within our remedy.
>
> « *Hamlet*, 2.2.10–18; Bevington, 1087 »

The moment Rosencrantz and Guildenstern accept this charge, they choose betrayal; they take sides, not with Hamlet by listening to him discreetly, but against him. They believe the account that the king and queen give of the change in Hamlet, and they accept the surface explanation for that change: the prince is mad. By adopting ordinary meanings and heeding the words of others rather than trusting in their own acquaintance with Hamlet and thinking it possible to understand him, they place themselves outside of the relationship; they betray their friendship.

On their arrival Hamlet seeks to offer his two friends an opportunity to escape from what he immediately senses is a betrayal:

But let me conjure you, by the rights of our fellowship, by the con-sonancy of our youth, by the obligation of our ever-preserv'd love, and by what more dear a better proposer could charge you withal, be even and direct with me, whether you were sent for, or no!

«*Hamlet*, 2.2.284–89; Bevington, 1090.»

Abandoning for a moment the mask of madness, Hamlet at-tempts to avert betrayal by appealing to the implicit pacts of loy-alty that underlie their friendship, to the affective ties that link-ed them, and, ultimately, to their harmony in the days they spent together and understood one another. Hamlet's appeal to them is a cry of desperation, a plea for comprehension and respect re-served for friends.

The two remain stolidly deaf to Hamlet's appeal because they fail to understand how deep it goes. In fact, Hamlet later says to Rosencrantz, "A knavish speech sleeps in a foolish ear" (*Hamlet*, 4.2.24–25; Bevington, 1105).

Because they fail to understand Hamlet's appeal to them, Rosencrantz and Guildenstern think a verbal admission—"My lord, we were sent for" (*Hamlet*, 2.2.293; Bevington, 1090)—suf-ficient to eliminate betrayal and assert their loyalty to him. But Hamlet has asked for something more than sincere words; he has asked for sincere souls; he has asked them to be fully present, to be with him.

The two friends admit that they were sent for, but they slide into treachery all the same, because they are in part with Hamlet and in part with the king and queen, who also have a claim on their loyalty. They are a bit here and a bit there. For them, Hamlet is now a madman, a danger, and it is their task to save him. Rosen-crantz and Guildenstern mistake the thrust of the king and queen's request, believing they were summoned to help their friend. Thanks to that misunderstanding, they think they are displaying their loyalty and obedience to their sovereigns, but the king and queen want only to make use of them against Ham-let. It is that misunderstanding that makes the two men deaf to the words of their friend the prince: they end up betraying him by failing to comprehend what he is saying. They do not truly listen to what Hamlet is saying to them but rather reinterpret his words and filter them through the prejudice instilled in their minds by the king and queen. They stand before Hamlet, but they do not stand with him; they betray both their communication with him and their former harmonious relationship.

For his part, Hamlet senses that his old companions, perhaps unwittingly, are betraying him. He senses that they are both reticent and indiscreet, intrusive and timorous, but above all he perceives that they have no desire to enter into genuine relations with him. Thus when the king orders him to go to England in the company of Rosencrantz and Guildenstern, Hamlet understands that they are being used to escort him to his death. Betrayed, he must then prepare himself to betray them:

> There's letters seal'd, and my two schoolfellows,
> Whom I will trust as I will adders fang'd,
> They bear the mandate; they must sweep my way,
> And marshal me to knavery. Let it work.
> For 'tis the sport to have the enginer
> Hoist with his own petar; and 't shall go hard
> But I will delve one yard below their mines,
> And blow them at the moon.

« *Hamlet*, 3.4.209–16; Bevington, 1104 »

Hamlet manages to gain possession of the message that the two friends are to hand over to the king of England in which the king of Denmark asks his English counterpart to kill the young prince immediately, and he substitutes an order to kill Rosencrantz and Guildenstern, thus making sure that the "enginer" will be "hoist with his own petar" and that the two betrayers will be betrayed. Rosencrantz and Guildenstern are unaware of the content of the letter that has been entrusted to them, which means that their betrayal does not consist in consciously deceiving Hamlet, but rather in blindly obeying the king's orders without taking the trouble to ascertain Hamlet's desires or thoughts— which he, of course, keeps carefully concealed. In a certain sense,

Hamlet is the victim of his own secrecy and his mistrust of his old school companions. It is a mistrust that is confirmed, however, by the ambiguous and ambivalent attitude of Rosencrantz and Guildenstern, who oscillate between two loyalties, one to their sovereigns and one to their friend. Being both *here and there* leads them to the betrayal and to their own ruin.

Although Hamlet does not kill them in a physical sense, he writes their death order and arranges for their assassination. This means that Hamlet, too, is strongly ambivalent: he scorns his old friends, but he still feels some affection for them; he prepares their death, but he relates it to Horatio as an inevitable destiny that must be fulfilled. In his own eyes, he is not the one who has betrayed: Rosencrantz and Guildenstern are guilty of betrayal because they had understood nothing of what was happening around them. They died for their own foolish ignorance, not because of Hamlet's betrayal of them:

> Why, man, they did make love to this employment;
> They are not near my conscience. Their defeat
> Does by their own insinuation grow.
> 'Tis dangerous when the baser nature comes
> Between the pass and fell incensed points
> Of mighty opposites.

« *Hamlet*, 5.2.57–62; Bevington, 1116 »

Rosencrantz and Guildenstern die the victims of too many secrets and of events too big for them: Hamlet's secret, which they never do understand; the secret of the king, who uses them as his instruments; and their own secret pact of alliance with the king.

Betrayers, they are also betrayed—because they gave up trying to understand, because they were so witless, because they lightly abandoned their affective ties to Hamlet, because they preferred acceptance of the commonplace meaning of words to the arduous task of discovering what lay behind them, because they had never been completely present in their relationship with the prince.

Only after Hamlet himself has been killed can his secrets be told. At that point there is no reason to conceal his thoughts, and in fact they must be revealed if his memory is to survive after his death. Horatio, who has shared those secrets, is the only one who can reveal them. As the young prince lies dying, he begs Horatio not to follow him in death but to keep on living in order to tell his tale:

> O God, Horatio, what a wounded name,
> Things standing thus unknown, shall I leave behind me!
> If thou didst ever hold me in thy heart,
> Absent thee from felicity awhile,
> And in this harsh world draw thy breath in pain
> To tell my story.
>
> «*Hamlet*, 5.2.346–51; Bevington, 1120)»

Hamlet knows that Horatio alone can tell that story. He has not only been a witness to it but a conscious actor in Hamlet's drama; he has been focused on discerning and understanding what was happening and on comprehending how such tragic events came to be mingled with "accidental judgments, casual slaughters"; how calculated, self-interested betrayals came to be intertwined with absurd betrayals (such as that of Rosencrantz and Guildenstern) for no genuine reason. Horatio winds up the story:

> And let me speak to th' yet unknowing world
> How these things came about. So shall you hear
> Of carnal, bloody, and unnatural acts,
> Of accidental judgments, casual slaughters,
> Of deaths put on by cunning and forc'd cause,
> And, in this upshot, purposes mistook
> Fall'n on th' inventors' heads. All this can I
> Truly deliver.
>
> «*Hamlet*, 5.2.381–88; Bevington, 1120»

5

The Culture of Betrayal: From the Tudors to the Internet

Natures of such deep trust we shall much need.
«SHAKESPEARE, *King Lear*, 2.1.117; Bevington, 1185»

Betrayal as a Sin and as a Resource

Every epoch and every society produces particular forms of betrayal with differing judgments and evaluations of it and differing moral and social sanctions against it. Even moving from one social level to another or from one subculture to another can result in changes in the definition and evaluation of betrayal. For example, in some social circles and some subcultures, marital infidelity is condemned without appeal, whereas in others the very notion of infidelity does not exist, because love relationships are based on an absolute and reciprocal freedom.

Strongly ideological or religious social organizations, whose culture is based on faith in the existence of an absolute truth, tend to condemn and punish severely all forms of betrayal. Treachery in fact threatens a symbolic order in which affiliation and a sense of cohesion are all-important and leave no room for ambivalence or deviation.

We can hypothesize that the various forms of betrayal, public and private, are more widespread in transitional phases and times of instability or social change. In such moments uncertainty casts doubt not only on social identities but on personal identities, as individuals are obliged to redefine criteria, judgments, and alliances and to make choices, take sides, and take a position regarding the world and themselves. This process of redefinition inevitably includes abandonments and desertions as people move from one affiliation to another and seize opportunities for betrayal.

Marx's dictum "All that is solid melts into air, and all that is holy is profaned" refers to the turmoil that modernization produces, both in interpersonal relations and social relations.[1] Everything vanishes into thin air because old affiliations no longer count for much. Connections, promises, and oaths can and must be broken in the name of the new order.

Betrayal becomes more frequent in phases of intense social mobility, especially where they concern previous social groups, lifestyles, friendship circles, and affective ties. All of Honoré de Balzac's novels, from *Père Goriot* to *Les illusions perdues,* are tales of betrayal—of a determined struggle for advancement that leaves in its wake the destruction of all previous ties and affiliations.[2]

Until the rise and consolidation of the modern state, betrayal had been used as a means, if not frankly a resource, for resolving public and personal problems. Public treachery was often intertwined with private: betrayal among kin (as with Richard III) or between friends (as in *Macbeth*) was predictable and considered inevitable whenever power was at stake. The events in Shakespeare's plays and in Elizabethan theater in general reflect a society in which betrayal was part of both the political game and interpersonal relations. In Tudor England, given the absence of any guarantee of individual liberty and the intense personalization of political struggles, a mere accusation of betrayal was enough to justify assassinations and vendettas.

Until the arrival of the modern age, betrayals of the homeland, the sovereign, or one's own kin were so commonplace that they were almost predictable. Even though a culture of suspicion and conspiracy strongly conditioned both public and private behavior, betrayal was nonetheless considered shameful and the most unpardonable of sins. Although betrayal was a social practice and a form of interpersonal relations deeply embedded in everyday life, it was still held to be a grave fault. Until the late sixteenth century, that apparent contradiction—that contrast between behavior and the judgment of it—can probably be explained by the influence of religious explanations. Although betrayal was omnipresent, it remained a high offense against God: to threaten the existent public and social order was a threat to the divine order. Conspiring against the king, like betraying a friend or a relation, was a sin, and for that reason could be severely punished.

Although betrayal was present at every hand, this did not eliminate ties of fidelity: as Shklar writes, treachery always "included . . . 'the corruption' of the blood of the traitor."[3] Betrayal called into question values held to be basic in societies of the time: honor, conjugal fidelity, loyalty in friendship, obedience to one's lord. For that reason as well, treachery, although widespread and frequent, was considered the most terrible of ills.

Moral condemnation remained as severe in the late sixteenth century as it had been in the age of Dante Alighieri. Dante refers to traitors as a "misbegotten rabble of all rabble" (sovra tutte mal creata plebe), and he places them in the lowest circle of Hell, immersed up to their necks in a vast frozen lake. These are the sinners who most closely approach absolute evil and who are placed nearest to Lucifer, the betrayer of God. Dante reserves his harshest words for political traitors because they destroy social harmony by stirring up feuds and discord, even within the family. This is why he portrays them still focused on accusing one another, even in Hell, as is the case of Bocca degli Abati, who would prefer to be forgotten but is unmasked before Dante by another of the damned traitors.[4]

Attitudes toward betrayal changed with the rise of modern political theory. Machiavelli was the first to break with tradition: he gave betrayal a new dimension by including it within a secular explanation and interpretation of the world. In all of his works, but in *The Prince* and the *Discourses* in particular, Machiavelli considers treachery to be a legitimate means for obtaining and maintaining power, but also (and in particular) as a novel way to manage power. That innovation, Machiavelli seems to suggest, results from a breakup of symbolic orders and from gaps caused by the shift from old to new forms of the administration of power. Precisely because betrayal is disruptive and destructive of ties, alliances, and shared experiences, it is not so much simply one means among others available for the realization of an aim but the most symbolically efficacious way to do so.

Keeping one's word and honoring trust are not virtues to be praised in the abstract, Machiavelli tells us. Rather, they are to be used when and if the situation so demands. If a new prince finds that the salvation of the state and the maintenance of government require deceits and betrayals, he should use them without hesitation:

> A prudent lord, therefore, cannot observe faith, nor should he, when such observance turns against him, and the causes that made him promise have been eliminated. . . . But it is necessary to know well how to color this nature, and to be a great pretender and dissembler; and men are so simple and so obedient to present necessities that he who deceives will always find someone who will let himself be deceived.[5]

Pope Alexander VI made constant use of betrayal and deceit, and Machiavelli says of him that "his deceits succeeded at his will, because he well knew this aspect of the world."[6] When betrayal was detached from ethics and religion, it became one of many possible behaviors and an available resource.

Betrayal, along with its corollaries, deceit and dissimulation, were inserted into a secular symbolic universe in which they received something like legitimation during the course of the seventeenth century. That was in fact the century of treatises on the need for lying and on the art of prudence, understood as a talent for dissimulation (as in Baldassare Gracian's treatise, *The Art of*

Worldly Wisdom[7]), of theatrical representations of liars and seducers (Tirso De Molina's *Don Juan* emerged from that same culture), of the pictorial art of *trompe l'oeil*, and of Torquato Accetto's treatise on "honest" dissimulation, *Della dissimlazione onesta*. As it became established, baroque culture drew a connection between liberty, inner autonomy, and an ability to deceive and betray that provided the basis for a culture of modern subjectivity that holds that deceit and artifice are necessary to the affirmation of individuality and the tutelage of what Torquato Accetto calls "the secret house of the heart":

> We admire it as a sign of the greatness of men of high estate when they remain in the deep recesses of palaces and the secret chambers therein, surrounded by iron and by men who guard their persons and their interests, but it is nonetheless clear that, without so much expenditure, every man, even though he is exposed to the gaze of all, can conceal his affairs in the vast but also secret house of his heart, because that is where those serene temples that Lucretius sang of are located.[8]

Secrecy provided a foundation for baroque man: under cover and in silence, it set him free. For better or for worse, as Salvatore Silvano Nigro writes in his introduction to Accetto's treatise, the culture of individual liberty swept away the ethics of sincerity and loyalty, replacing it with an ethics based on an inner and personal responsibility.[9] Individuality found further support in an enhanced ability to resist oppressive laws, rules, and powers that limited the autonomy of the conscience and freedom of judgment.

Accetto's treatise was first published in 1641, but it was rediscovered and republished by Benedetto Croce in 1928, three centuries later, when it was read as an anti-Fascist tract. As Nigro emphasizes, "It was reprinted, this time in polemic with the Fascist dictatorship, because in a regime of lies there is a delicate and risky boundary between the sufferings of an inner liberty when it hides the truth and the bad faith of not being sincere with oneself."[10]

The affirmation of an ethics of dissimulation, viewed as an ethics of fidelity to oneself and to individual responsibility, introduced a changed evaluation of betrayal. "Not to betray oneself" became the new moral imperative, and on its altar betrayal of the other became a rite of sacrifice to the affirmation of individual identity. It is thus in the seventeenth century that we find the tightly interwoven roots of the new subjectivity, of a culture of the individual, and of a moral and social tolerance of betrayal. The notions of both the individual and of individuality had changed, and the bourgeois subject of the modern age, a contradictory being with no outstanding qualities, replaced the heroic *chevalier sans peur et sans reproche.*

Modernity and Betrayal

What are the forms of betrayal in the early modern age and after? How has it been evaluated? And what sanctions have been connected with it?

In modern times, political upheavals, changes of government, and alliances between states are no longer achieved through betrayal, but rather by using the resources of politics and democracy. Naturally, betrayals and betrayers continue to exist, but, unlike the use of betrayal in the premodern world, when—in much the same way as war—it was the prime means for change, betrayal came to be used as one among several means for realizing political, personal, or collective goals.

With the growth of the central state and its power to monopolize violence, punishment for betrayal of the homeland (treason), attempted coups d'état, and political conspiracies has shifted from personal vendettas on the part of groups or factions that felt themselves betrayed to being punishable only by representatives of the state. In modern times, public betrayal loses its personal character; it is now punished severely as a crime against institutions rather than against the person at the head of the government, be he president of the republic, king, or general of the army. Treason, as Shklar notes, is the only crime mentioned in the Constitution of the United States. In Great Britain as well, a major law regarding public order pertains to treason: "Treason is the most serious crime offense against the state and as such it carries the mandatory sentence of the death penalty." Shklar continues, "In both countries, levying war against the state and adhering to its enemies and giving them aid and comfort are, as they have always been, at the center of public treachery."[11]

With the establishment of individual guarantees, the crime of betrayal and the accusation of high treason could no longer be used as weapons of political struggle, except in dictatorships. Treason becomes punishable only in the presence of certain proof, as stated in Article III, Section 2 of the Constitution of the United States: "No person shall be convicted of Treason unless on the testimony of two Witnesses to the same Overt Act, or on Confession in open court."[12]

The reasoning behind this provision is to prevent the accusation of treason from being used to threaten or destroy institutional guarantees and individual liberties. When betrayal of the homeland and public betrayals are evoked too often and punished too severely, there is a danger of losing all guarantees of personal liberty: "At all times and in all places . . . the skeptical intelligence must intervene, to restrain despair, to prevent general misanthropy, and above all to stop the destruction of a liberal order that is too determined to avenge itself upon its betrayers."[13]

With the shift to modern times, public betrayal has taken on a different social significance. In losing its function as a political instrument, it has also lost much of its moral infamy, and it is no longer punished by private vendetta.

Modern times have brought a clearer distinction between the public and the private spheres and, especially in a period of greater social complexity, a decrease in social control and an increase in individual liberty have made the private betrayals of everyday life both more common and better tolerated. With the affirmation of individual responsibility and a respect for individual choices and with the erosion of such values as honor and loyalty, which are no longer the foundation of social organization, moral and social sanctions against betrayal have tended to disappear almost entirely.

In the premodern world, to betray meant primarily to fail to live up to codes of honor and fidelity, norms of behavior, and rituals that rigidly regulated social and interpersonal relations. In the modern world betrayal relates to the individual conscience: it is an infraction of rules regarding sentiments and personal interactions. What is attacked by betrayal is no longer a system of rules or a code, but rather the single individual and the specific relationship. Individuals freely choose to exchange promises and swear to loyalty pacts, implicit or explicit, and they can break their word just as freely without having general values and codes of honor and loyalty enter into the picture. Someone who betrays is guilty only of having damaged a particular relationship, and betrayal is and can be judged as an event that concerns only the persons involved. Praise of such values as loyalty and honor and calling for innately loyal men—as the Duke of Cornwall says when he comes to the aid of the aged King Lear, "Natures of such deep trust we shall much need"—were justifiable in a social reality in which pacts and alliances needed to be proclaimed sacred because personal survival and survival of the social order were connected to the benevolence or the caprice of a lord and his clan.

Trust and loyalty were resources that united groups and persons against other groups or factions; thus, they were qualities treated with solemnity and invested with exclusivity. With the shift to the modern age, "notions of personal or social trust moved from highly charged, exclusivistic codes to calmer, more routinized and universal ones."[14]

As Allan Silver stresses here, the emotional charge that had accompanied the idea of trust up to the late eighteenth century tended to vanish afterward, precisely because in those earlier days exclusive and personal relations were founded on trust and loyalty. What we see now is a secularization of trust. Like benevolence, sympathy, or prudence, it has become a resource available for spending—a widely shared attitude without exclusivist implications.

With the institution of laws and regulations that disregard personal ties, both betrayal as a possible resource and the sacredness attached to loyalty disappear. To betray or to be betrayed becomes an increasingly private affair in the realm of intersubjectivity, while political betrayal becomes uniquely public and has little or no personal or moral implications attached to it. But precisely because pacts and explicit or implicit promises of loyalty are put into effect freely, it is the expectations specific to the relationship—of love, friendship, or kinship—that are disappointed and ignored when promises are broken.

Although loyal behavior is still considered necessary, that loyalty results more from social practices, individual decisions, and innate good manners than from the "natures of such deep trust" that Cornwall invokes in *King Lear*. To be loyal is no longer a question of rank; loyalty is not a product of noble birth or a noble soul. More democratically, it is a choice that any individual can make, freely and according to his preferences, judgments, and notions of propriety. To be loyal no longer implies an exclusive affiliation: just as one can be a member of more than one group, one can have more than a single loyalty, choosing instead the loyalty that seems most compelling at a given moment.

Social Complexity and Betrayal

Increased social complexity has brought on a proliferation of interpersonal relations that are fast becoming more impersonal. It is increasingly difficult to claim to be sons or daughters of one homeland or citizens of one country. For everyone there is at least the possibility of a "world elsewhere." We are all exiles and we are all alone, but at the same time we are deeply caught within vast networks of communication and collaboration. We do not totally belong to anyone, but rather have many relationships on which our public and private lives depend. We also owe our lives to the fact that we can trust in many unknown persons, and we set down roots, ephemerally but necessarily, in every local situation (taken in either the purely spatial sense or the relational sense) in which we find ourselves interacting.

According to Simmel, in the modern age trusting that we will not be deceived becomes a fundamental resource without which we can make no decisions and take no initiatives, because it is increasingly true that we do not know, except perhaps superficially, those with whom we interact. By the same token, we interact less and less with the people we do know, and the people we rely on become more and more numerous. Precisely because we cannot know all of these people in any deep sense, however, and although we trust them, we reserve a corner of our minds for an awareness that they can disappoint or betray us. We trust with caution and out of necessity.

The possibility of betrayal takes its place among the many and unpredictable forms that relationships can assume. Through this type of everyday experience, the subject in the modern age discovers the uncertainty lodged in every relationship, even in his or her own inner multiplicity and ambiguity. Not only can the other betray us, but we too can betray others. For Simmel, in human interaction "psychological knowledge ... depends ... upon the forms which the cognizing mind brings to it and in which it receives the given." In other words, psychological knowledge depends on the specific performance that the individual is giving.[15]

Modern life is based on a belief in the honesty of others, because we are obliged to rely on functions that only they can perform and notions that they possess. As Niklas Luhmann suggests, we have trust in order to reduce the complexity of modern society.[16] Honesty and loyalty are no longer taken to be fundamental personal virtues utterly necessary for social interaction and social cohesion. Rather, they are instruments needed to keep the motors of society running smoothly.

In other words, what it takes to keep the machinery of society humming is to think and act as if honesty and loyalty existed. The single individual is no longer expected to be consistently honest and loyal; it is enough to be so intermittently, according to need. In the modern age we learn to believe and trust partially, one specific interaction at a time, and only insofar as it is necessary to the construction, affirmation, and realization of individuality.

Faced with complexity, risk, and unpredictability, the individual has to choose between two different defensive strategies. The first consists in the creation of collaboration networks, systems of cooperation and mutual support that help to form systems of trust in which we can participate and within which we feel at least partially secure. These circuits of trust reinforce and reproduce themselves as long as our "trust in trust" is not betrayed. We choose strategically not to betray the trust placed in us so that the trust that we have placed in others will not be betrayed. We make ourselves trustworthy—just as we trust others—one sector at a time. Once again, trust and loyalty are not degrees of virtue; rather, they are instrumental and partial behaviors.

The other route—and the other defensive strategy—consists in making use of deceit and betrayal should the occasion arise and we feel it opportune to do so. Here betrayal of trust is used as a shortcut for obtaining goods (material or nonmaterial), resources, or information that we are not sure we can obtain otherwise. This second strategy, like trust, is a way to reduce complexity.

These two different ways of reducing complexity—trusting in trust and betraying trust—are not mutually exclusive, however. In the life of every individual they can run parallel or become intertwined. The proliferation of social circles and the increased membership affiliations they offer greatly enhance each individual's opportunities for betrayal and his or her opportunities to betray.

It becomes harder and harder to be equally loyal to all, and conflicts that force us to choose between loyalties become increasingly frequent. Anyone who belongs to several worlds at once but to none of them wholly will be betrayed sooner or later. The actual betrayal and its proximate cause will be determined by life's vicissitudes, the life phase that an individual is passing through, a momentary interest, or that individual's own scale of priorities, which he sets for himself and continually redefines.

Having multiple memberships, which means multiple loyalties, has not only become common in everyday interpersonal experience, it also has become typical of our relations with institutions. This challenges loyalties and fidelities that had previously been taken for granted, such as those toward one's country or toward the state.

In 1985 Jonathan Pollard, a civilian intelligence analyst for the U.S. Navy, was charged with passing information to Israel. He was convicted on one count of espionage and, in 1986, sentenced to life imprisonment. In 1998 Israel formally acknowledged him as a bona fide agent and granted him Israeli citizenship. Pollard's supporters argued that he should be released because the information had been passed on to a country that was an ally of the United States and one that he perceived as his second homeland.

Pollard himself, writing from prison, justified his activities as an Israeli spy by comparing them to efforts to hide Jews in Europe during World War II, adding that he did not consider himself a traitor because he had acted for the benefit of the cultural and religious community of which he was a part. For Pollard and his supporters, his dual affiliation and dual loyalty were justified and legitimate.

The situation was quite different in 1950, when Julius and Ethel Rosenberg were convicted of espionage. Although the Rosenbergs' conviction raised some objections regarding anti-Semitism, the problem of dual affiliation did not come up. The reasons for this change lie not only in the profound historical and political differences between the two acts of espionage or between the cold war atmosphere and the anti-Communism of the 1950s. I believe that the increasing relevance attributed nowadays to religious, ethnic, and gender identities has somehow encouraged a culture of affiliation and loyalty, but that at the same time the notion of a multiple self that can continuously choose his or her own affiliation lends legitimacy to the possibility of plural affiliations and betrayal.

As the question of the independence of the province of Quebec shows, one can be Canadian but also—and above all—be

Quebecois. Similarly, one can be Italian but feel oneself primarily *padano*—a native of the Po Valley—or American with a primary loyalty to being Jewish or, in a gender-based self-image, essentially female, and so forth. Once we begin counting off our possible memberships and identities and put them in an order determined by subjective criteria, it becomes harder to understand what or whom we are betraying. The very concept of betrayal begins to lose meaning. From this point of view, Pollard's defense seems less bizarre (as it did to Peter Beinert in an indignant contribution to the *New York Times* early in 1999) and instead becomes an interesting sign of an established culture of dual loyalties.[17]

What happens to the ties of loyalty and relations of trust that bind individuals to institutions and to their country? Does the advent of plural affiliations threaten the seemingly unbreakable connection between citizenship and loyalty to one's country? As the culture of betrayal and the culture of loyalty change, not only interpersonal relations but also relations between the individual and society come to be redefined.

If we turn to the problem of plural membership in a number of social circles, we see that each group in which an individual participates forms a We. Each of these groups provides opportunities to share secrets, areas of competence, sentiments, goals, promises, rites, lifestyles, and values. Only rarely do the full contents of this shared experience pertain to one We. It is harder and harder to share everything with one person, even in the most intimate relationships: "The modern way of feeling tends more heavily toward differentiated friendships, which cover only one side of the personality, without playing into other aspects of it. . . . Except for their earliest years, personalities are perhaps too uniquely individualized to allow full reciprocity of understanding and receptivity."[18]

If this is true of relations of friendship and love, it is all the more true of the infinite number of impersonal relations in which we are involved, day after day, and in which sharing is ever more particularized and more ephemeral. With friends, one's own group of equals, or even alone with one friend, we tend to share a lifestyle, but not values, or else we share sentiments, emotions, and rites, but not necessarily lifestyles. A group of friends can even be formed with no goal in mind and no common objective except the relationship itself. Or a We of friendship can be based on a common goal or shared secrets but still imply no shared values or sentiments.

A We made up of individuals in the same profession can be based on shared skills, rituals, objectives, and professional secrets and still exclude values, common lifestyles, affective complicities, or ideological choices. A We is formed in many ways and can implicate us in a variety of loyalty pacts and trust relations, and everyone who is involved in any form of sharing expects it to reflect particular and sectoral loyalties. We trust others and entrust ourselves to others only for the segments of our lives that we share for the time being.

The protagonist of one of Italo Calvino's short stories finds himself moving, indifferently and by whim, between a band of burglars and a group of policemen who are trying to catch them. He joins first one side, then the other, but he belongs to neither. His presence on one side or the other is always a matter of chance. For that reason, although he seems a traitor playing a double game, in reality he betrays no one because he shares no ties with either group and is only accidentally a member of one or the other. Calvino writes:

> I stopped to watch them.
>
> They were working, at night, in a secluded street, doing something with the shutter of a shop.
>
> It was a heavy shutter: they were using an iron bar for a lever, but the shutter wouldn't budge.
>
> I was walking around, going nowhere in particular, on my own. I got hold of the bar to give them a hand. They made room for me.

When the protagonist finds himself with the band of robbers, he helps them to raise the shutter, sharing their labors, their aim, and even their language: "'As long as those skunky police don't turn up!' they were saying. . . . I shook my head. 'Kill 'em all, that's what,' I answered."

At this point he unexpectedly and fortuitously changes sides. The robbers send him to check on the whereabouts of the police: "Outside, at the corner, there were others hugging the wall, hidden in the doorways, coming towards me. I joined in."

Calvino's protagonist has now gone over to the side of the police, collaborating with them and acting like one of them. In the course of this short narrative he changes sides several times, until finally the police burst into the shop while he is taking the side of the robbers:

We crouched down behind something, pale, grasping each other's hands. The others came into the backroom, didn't see us, turned round. We shot out and ran like crazy. "We've done it!" we shouted. I tripped a couple of times and got left behind. I found myself with the others running after them.

"Come on," they said, "we're catching up."

And everybody raced through the narrow streets, chasing them. "Run this way, cut through there," we said and the others weren't far ahead now, so that we were shouting: "Come on, they won't get away."

I managed to catch up with one of them. He said: "Well done, you got away. Come on, this way, we'll lose them." And I went along with him. After a while I found myself alone, in an alley. Someone came running round a corner and said: "Come on, this way, I saw them. They can't have gone far." I ran after him a while.

Then I stopped, in a sweat. There was no one left, I couldn't hear any more shouting. I stood with my hands in my pockets and started to walk, on my own, going nowhere in particular.[19]

The main figure in this story collaborates with both groups, interacting with their members and responding to their expectations when he is among them. As he shifts from one side to the other he reveals no secrets, passes no information. Still, precisely because he conforms to the behavior of one team, he acts against the other. He switches from one We to the other casually, for no given reason. He blends into one We and then into the other, and his sharing is purely situational and theatrical, in the sense that he participates in one staged version of what is taking place—that of the robbers—and then in the other—that of the police. In Goffman's terms, he is not a traitor because as long as he is with one group, he collaborates actively in its performance, supporting it and investing all his efforts and his loyalty in it. What he does when he is no longer with that group has no relevance or meaning, and he can be judged only from the standpoint of the rival performance. The betrayal—if indeed any betrayal is involved—lies in his incomplete affiliation, in the fact that he is never completely and definitively present. His betrayal is the diffuse and constant betrayal that is part of the solitude and the irreducible singularity of the modern subject.

Beyond the here and now, there seems no longer to be any way to account for our acts, no reason or motivation that explains them. Calvino's short story, significantly titled "Solidarity," is a metaphor for the modern condition and for an identity that is defined haphazardly from one situation to another. Calvino's tale opens and closes with his protagonist walking around the town on his own, "going nowhere in particular."

Solidarity and betrayal are interchangeable; they are both fortuitous, fleeting, and based on the experience of being wanderers, never setting down roots.

Even the economy and labor in our current phase of globalization are organized on the basis of flexibility, an ability to adapt to continual change, and the relative unimportance of all long-term commitments. Adopting the short term, change, and flexibility as organizational models is also reflected in everyday behavior and the definition of identity. In order for relations of trust, loyalty, and commitment to develop, we need long-lasting relationships and long-term experiences: we need to feel that we have roots. Given that being rooted is no longer functional (Richard Sennett laments the fact that it is even perceived as an obstacle), there is less chance of founding relations of trust and of developing loyalty and affection, either with individuals or organizations and institutions. Anyone who has to be ready to change occupation, organization, or residence or to be expelled from the labor market no longer has the leisure to develop lasting relationships or deep-rooted loyalties. This not only undermines an identity that has also become flexible, always ready to adapt to new conditions and never setting down roots (which, incidentally, makes it difficult for any individual to narrate his or her own story as a series of conscious choices), it also makes it impossible to transmit to our children such values as loyalty, fidelity, commitment, and affection.

One young manager whom Sennett interviewed speaks about the demand for flexibility and its influence on his family life: "You can't imagine how stupid I feel when I talk to my kids about commitment. It's an abstract virtue to them; they don't see it anywhere."[20]

For Sennett, the "no long term" imperative corrodes both the individual and the collective experience of forms of trust that go beyond the minimal level of the simple trust required to maintain business relations: "Trust can, of course, be a purely formal matter, as when people agree to a business deal or rely on another to observe the rules in a game. But usually deeper experiences of trust are more informal, as when people learn on whom they can rely when given a difficult or impossible task. Such social bonds take time to develop, slowly rooting into the cracks and crevices of institutions."[21]

One Option among Many

When an attack is mounted on the shared elements or objectives of a particular We, to the point of threatening the relationship itself or of disappointing expectations, we can speak of betrayal as having a social role, rather than as a morally or socially contemptible act. If an individual betrays a professional We by revealing a secret or not participating in the achievement of a goal set by the group or institution, he will be labeled as professionally undependable, a judgment that pertains more to the act than to the person. There will be talk of betrayal and disloyalty, but the individual will probably not be considered a traitor or inherently untrustworthy. Even eventual sanctions will remain within the professional or social circle within which the supposed fault was committed. In other settings that individual will continue to enjoy esteem and trust, even if his questionable professional conduct should come to be known. He will probably be considered a good citizen, a good husband, and a faithful friend. Complete freedom and personal responsibility is taken for granted in every We in which we take part. No one invests all of himself or herself in one We, which means that people can betray one of the many groups in which they participate because they are sure of a "social indifference" that guarantees a sort of immunity, and they know that they can count on the continued trust of other membership groups. Social perception—the image of an individual that all of the other We groups not yet betrayed will have—will not be one of a traitor. Moreover, the subject himself will not feel himself to be a traitor, thanks to that immunity and to the "political asylum" that his other We groups will offer him. The individual who has betrayed in only one part of his complex social life can even enjoy a positive self-image. The social perception of betrayal and the moral judgment of it are more and more nuanced in a situation of social complexity, and they are increasingly circumscribed within particular areas or fragments of intersubjective life.

In this sense, betrayal becomes an increasingly common action (in all of the multiple meanings of the word *common*): it occurs daily, and it is an act that everyone commits sooner or later. This makes it more of a banal event than a tragic one. In a certain sense, betrayal becomes easier, not only because it has been freed from both external and internal sanctions but also because people can always construct, or think they can construct, another We. The illusion of being able to live more than one life history reinforces the chance that betrayal will be seen as banal rather than blameworthy—as a sign of personal liberty.

A culture is coming into being in which every individual can be judged only within a particular sphere of affiliation, because, among other reasons, we tend to ignore—whether out of indifference or discretion—how every member of a group, a We, behaves in other contexts. Social differentiation makes it harder and harder to define betrayal, and norms of loyalty and expectations of trust are becoming increasingly sectoral and ill-defined.

There now seems to be general agreement that drawing up an overall definition of the betrayer is an impossible task. This is reflected in expressions and modes of speech that are becoming more and more frequent in both the media and interpersonal communications: "A hard worker, loyal to his companions and friends, but in love an incorrigible traitor"; "A fine person, a good father to his family, but absolutely untrustworthy in the workplace: so ambitious that he would betray his best friend."

As social circles proliferate, the number of opportunities for betrayal grows, but its significance is diluted, at least in terms of penal sanctions and moral judgments. Betrayal becomes not only more widespread, more accepted, and socially less dramatic; it also seems to meet with general indifference and to elude all categories of moral judgment.

One example of the loss of social relevance of betrayal and its acceptance as one possible mode of behavior that might, at most, offend sensibilities was the debate over whether President Clinton should be impeached. Debate centered on accusations of perjury, of making false statements under oath, rather than on the president's conjugal fidelity or any disloyalty he may have shown to his friends and supporters. His putative betrayal of his wife, his friends, and his closest collaborators was either the topic of jokes or was used by Republican politicians to weaken the figure of the president. A majority of Americans, as shown in a number of polls, justified the president's behavior either by stating that we are all capable of betrayal now and then, in particular in the form of marital infidelity, or that if there was any betrayal, it was Bill Clinton's own business. These were considered private matters, and many of those polled criticized the violation of the president's privacy. Republicans' efforts to stigmatize Clinton's conjugal betrayals by invoking family values and fidelity did little or nothing to change the opinion of the majority of Americans.

Much has changed in society—and thankfully so—from the time when Hester Prynne, the heroine of Nathaniel Hawthorne's *The Scarlet Letter*, was obliged to wear an "A" for adultery sewn to her clothing as a sign of moral unworthiness, to the time when presidential infidelities were met with indifference.

This shift is one sign of the modernization and secularization of American culture and of a growing separation between the public sphere and the private sphere, but from a sociological point of view it is also a sign of the decreased social relevance of conjugal betrayal and the betrayal of trust. Such betrayals become a strictly personal choice—one option among many.

What is more, little attention has been paid to the fact that the accusations and the evidence against Clinton were gathered thanks to Linda Tripp's betrayal of her friends. While Tripp was drawing out Monica Lewinsky or Kathleen Willey and playing the role of friend, she was preparing to use their confidences for her own purposes, going so far as to record some conversations in order to make political use of them. This was a glaring and radical betrayal of the bonds of friendship, perpetrated by deceitful means, but that aspect of the whole affair met with general indifference. In my opinion, Tripp's behavior could even be judged to be very clever and almost justified by Monica Lewinsky's ingenuous candor. None of the victims of Tripp's betrayal denounced it publicly, nor did they cite it to question Tripp's reliability or to demonstrate her untrustworthiness.

In short, the Tripp story provides one more sign that betrayal is increasingly acceptable from a social point of view as a "normal" mode of interaction and is increasingly considered an "ordinary vice."

Despite social indifference, however, betrayal remains a traumatic and painful experience for the people directly involved in it. It has a contradictory significance: although banal for society, betrayal remains a threat and a painful experience for the individual. We all stand alone with our betrayals. An awareness that we can be betrayed at every turn and that we remain alone with our own suffering only adds to the bitterness of the betrayal experience. Precisely because betrayal has lost social relevance and significance, there is a tendency to make little of it and minimize its effects when it happens to others. Betrayal becomes part of a symbolic universe that leaves it unexplained—not legitimated, but nonetheless accepted.

What can it mean to speak about betrayal today? Has it become just an intrapsychic experience? If so, what new meaning does betrayal take on for the betrayed and for the betrayer? How can the story of the betrayed be told when the narrator can find no way to express it? And how can the betrayer's act be narrated when it meets with a "no comment" rather than a judgment?

What name would Judas or Peter have given to their suffering if their betrayals had taken place amid general indifference?

"RL is just one more window"

Among the many possible forms of affiliation we now have to include the many discussion groups, multi-user domains, self-help sites, and search engines available on the Internet. Such groups, which attract an ever-larger number of members, provide a great many possible (albeit virtual) opportunities to form a We. Web navigators who choose to escape from the real world have available a broad range of membership groups and affiliations; they can construct relationships, love stories, and sexual adventures, secure in the knowledge that the computer screen protects them and enables them to select any identity they want. The self is multiplied to the nth power; we can present ourselves under different guises, construct an infinite number of identities, and invent a narrative for each one.

The fact that these various "We" groupings are virtual seems not to diminish either the sense of membership or the expectations of loyalty on the part of participants. They are unknown to one another, yet they trust in one another, united in and connected by the network. Early studies of interpersonal relations through the Internet have shown that every network group creates rules, expects members to respect those rules and show mutual trust, and tends to operate like a genuine community.[22] Affiliation, loyalty, trust, and betrayal seem to be reproduced even when communication is virtual, perhaps because the intersubjectivity that emerges from such groups is by no means virtual.

The reproduction not only of the real world's rules for behavior but also of its expectations (trust, loyalty) leads habitual Internet navigators to confuse the two realms, attributing the same valence to the virtual world and the real one.

"RL is just one more window," one of the people interviewed by the psychologist Sherry Turkle declares.[23] But if real life is just one of the many windows that we can open or close at will on the computer screen, every window that we choose to open becomes a form of reality in which we experience forms of intersubjectivity that resemble those of the real world. Thus we move from one window to another, from one world to another, from one life to another, and from one identity to another. If all windows are interchangeable forms of life, so is our membership in different worlds. This multiplies our chances of betraying one or another of those memberships and of becoming involved in conflicts of loyalty.

One extremely significant case, where a conflict of loyalties between the virtual world and the real world is concerned, is that of a woman who informed the authorities that a participant in her support group for recovering alcoholics had admitted, via the Internet, that he had killed his own daughter a few years earlier.[24] The man confessed to the crime, but the other participants in the group rallied to support the murderer, accusing the woman who had informed the police of having betrayed both their trust and Internet ethics by revealing to the outside world things that had been shared in the virtual world, that hence were subject to an implicit pact of secrecy.

The woman, Elisa DeCarlo, "said that she was horrified by the E-mail message, but she grew even more dismayed over the on-line debate that followed.... It seemed to Ms. DeCarlo that the nature of on-line communication—which creates a psychological as well as a physical distance between participants—was causing her on-line friends to forget their off-line responsibilities to bring a confessed murderer to justice."

She had betrayed the murderer in the etymological sense of *trādere* by informing the police and by transferring secrets and confessions from one side to the other, one world to the other. For the other members of the community it was irrelevant that the informer had learned that her silence regarding a horrible infanticide would have made her an accomplice in the crime, thus betraying the rules of nonvirtual society, where such crimes are inadmissible. Before DeCarlo made up her mind to inform the police about the murder, she had debated what was the right thing to do, gripped by a conflict of loyalty between the Internet community, in which she spent a good deal of her time, and society at large, in which she lived along with other citizens, Internet navigators or not. Thus separate rules exist for the Internet and for real life, and belonging to both worlds can produce conflicts of loyalty, given that one inevitably betrays one world or the other.

DeCarlo, the woman at the center of this controversy, can be defined as a traitor or not according to the world that is doing the judging, but there is little connection between their contradictory evaluations. For its navigators, betraying the Internet community was a serious crime, whereas they were indifferent to betraying the rules of the civil community. For the civil community, on the other hand, it matters little how the individual behaves and chooses to live in the virtual world.

Multiple affiliations are possible thanks to the fact that the norms regulating the Internet respect the secrecy of those who enter and participate in that world. It has recently been revealed, however, that secrecy has been violated in e-mail sites thought to be strictly reserved to users. When this occurs, users feel themselves betrayed, not so much by the persons or agencies that invade their private space, but rather by the system itself, which turns out to be incapable of keeping secrets. Consumers have launched a series of lawsuits against the companies that manage access to the Internet, accusing them of having betrayed users' trust.

One clamorous case of this sort was resolved in 1998, when a senior chief petty officer in the U.S. Navy, Tim McVeigh, was "outed" by a navy civilian employee who discovered that the word "gay" was part of his America Online profile (he had used a screen name, but AOL revealed his real full name). Once "outed," McVeigh was separated from the navy because he had broken the unwritten law of the armed forces of the United States, according to which homosexuals can serve only if they agree not to make any public declaration of their sexual orientation. The other side of the bargain is for the armed forces to not ask questions about a recruit's sexual preferences. Both sides commit themselves to respect a "don't ask, don't tell" policy.

McVeigh respected this rule, and he appeared as a homosexual only in the virtual world. He was confident that there his personal information would be protected and inaccessible to outsiders, and that America Online would respect its promise of privacy, secrecy, and confidentiality.

Thus McVeigh's expectations of trust were betrayed on many counts. The navy had not respected its own "don't ask" rule, thus betraying an implicit pact. By violating a commitment explicitly stated in its subscription contract, which guarantees absolute confidentiality, America Online betrayed the trust of all users of its system. But when McVeigh trusted in the rules of the virtual world, he betrayed the rules of the navy, his real-world community, in turn failing to respect the "don't tell" rule by declaring online that he was gay. In the end the navy was obligated to reinstate McVeigh, and America Online agreed to pay damages to him. AOL also promised never again to reveal personal information about its subscribers. McVeigh's right to be himself in the virtual world was thus recognized, at least where his sexual orientation was concerned, but so was his right to be an officer of no stated sexuality within the world of the United States Navy. His dual affiliations—membership in the gay world online and in the navy in the real world—were thus recognized both juridically and socially. This affair confirms the possibility of being both here and elsewhere and the existence of parallel but different identities. It also reinforces the separation between virtual reality and the real world.

The perception that communications via the Internet are by no means abstract makes it true that behaviors both trustworthy and untrustworthy (which also means trustworthiness and betrayal) have not disappeared from the dynamics of interpersonal relations. This is why we trust and expect trustworthiness even from people we do not know. The projection of values and behaviors from the real world onto life on the screen transforms the virtual world into a world endowed with emotions and expectations. This determines the transfer of models of behavior, emotions, and affective relations from the real world to the virtual world. Not surprisingly, both women and men are highly jealous of their partners' online relationships, and they consider excessive chat-group interchanges or e-mails with another person, seen as a genuine rival, to be a true betrayal.

This personalization of apparently impersonal communications that involve emotions and the affective sphere leads to utterly traditional judgments and behaviors. The women suspect their partners of using the Internet to pursue relations with other women, and men, too, are jealous of their partners' virtual relations. Paradoxically, the gender of both the person who sends a message and the one who responds are undefined. This leads to the thought that life on the computer screen is lived—both by the user and by the person who shares his or her everyday life or has an affective relation with the user—as "a world elsewhere," a different world counterposed to the "real We," hence as another We.

A poll regarding couples and the Internet taken in Italy by the polling company Meta Srl, based on the opinions of 342 married Italian women and reported in the June 2000 issue of the periodical *Internet pratico*, found that 40 percent of these wives feared that their partner might have relations through the Internet with women more intelligent and more attractive than they. According to this report, "One out of every two women, or 49 percent of the women interviewed, is subject to a genuine attack of jealousy every time her partner or husband connects with the

Internet. . . . An excessive attachment to the computer, but to the Internet in particular, irritates 64 percent of the wives interviewed, whereas only 9 percent declare themselves unconcerned."

The fact that nothing can be known about who the Internet contact—male or female—might be undoubtedly adds to a sense of panic and exclusion, inviting the worst fantasies that can go along with jealousy and a feeling of being betrayed. Supposed online infidelities invite us to reflect on betrayal as something that eludes purely material definition, and they suggest that what is perceived as removal or flight from the We also includes the sphere of emotions and fantasies. Whether or not the other—male or female—actually has an amorous relationship or sexual relations outside the couple is less important than the fact that such a possibility leads to fantasizing about other forms of intimacy and another possible We. Jealousy and the perception of betrayal aroused by an awareness that one's partner is imagining different forms of intimacy existed long before the Internet. Literary examples abound: to pick one, there is Arthur Schnitzler's novel, *Traumnovelle* (translated in English as *Rhapsody: A Dream Novel*), which Stanley Kubrick took as the inspiration for his film *Eyes Wide Shut.*

In 1998 the *New York Times Magazine* carried the following story.[25] A group of wives who suspected their husbands of infidelity asked a private detective to obtain information on them via the Internet. The detective discovered that at least some of the husbands had been soliciting encounters—and not just online encounters—with women they did not know, and he also gained access to their secret amorous e-mail correspondence. On the basis of the evidence collected in these piracy operations, some of the wives filed for and obtained a divorce. The betraying husbands were in turn betrayed by the Internet, where they had felt secure but which turned out to be highly unreliable. Originally the accused, they became the accusers. This case, and many other cases of betrayal in virtual space, prompted wide debate about Internet rules and about behaviors that should or should not be permitted on the Web. What is under debate is thus no longer marital fidelity or interpersonal loyalty but rather the relations between a system of communication and its users. What is in crisis is a systematic trust that had seemed universally accepted in the late-modern world.[26] Society's focus on betrayal has thus shifted from an evaluation of personal loyalty to an evaluation of the credibility and trustworthiness of a system.

The Internet has created new opportunities for betrayal and new modes of betrayal. These include betrayals made possible by the fact that users can conceal their identities; betrayals on the part of the system toward its users; and betrayals of the rules of the real world because users inhabit a new world that has its own norms.

Are the fluid rules of the virtual world what enables us to flit from one window to another, one loyalty to another? Or can we betray so lightly because the real world no longer seems to need "natures of such deep trust"? What meaning does responsibility toward the other have if we can all be "one, no one, and one hundred thousand," be both here and elsewhere? Thanks to the Web, a new and portable responsibility seems to be coming into being, a "laptop responsibility" that can move from window to window. Or can we imagine a responsibility valid within both worlds, in the Web and in real life?

All of these questions invite us to rethink such terms as loyalty, trust, and betrayal, given that our experience of them becomes ever more complex and that thus far there is no tradition to protect and teach us. We are the first generation of Internet navigators, the first to have the everyday physical experience of being both here and elsewhere.

Are we the first generation of a new species of betrayers? Lighthearted, flighty traitors devoid of self-awareness?

Or will a new sense of responsibility emerge from the suffering and the pain that affects the betrayed, if only on the computer screen? Abandonment and rejection still strike directly at the heart. Will the persistence of the pain connected with relationships betrayed—relationships that are never virtual because they involve passions and emotions—make it possible for our multiple and bruised identities to stir themselves to vigilance and to make use of being here and being elsewhere as an expansion of experience—as a cognitive and emotional enrichment that enables us, even when fully aware of the implications, to learn to live with betrayal?

Notes

INTRODUCTION
1. Tony Tanner, *Adultery in the Novel: Contract and Transgression* (Baltimore: Johns Hopkins University Press, 1984); in Italian translation as *L'adulterio nel romanzo* (Genoa: Marietti, 1990). 2. Judith N. Shklar, *Ordinary Vices* (Cambridge: Harvard University Press, Belknap Press, 1984); in Italian translation as *Vizi comuni* (Bologna: Il Mulino, 1986). 3. See Karl Abraham et al., *Bugiardi e traditori* (Turin: Bollati Boringhieri, 1994).

CHAPTER ONE
Epigraph. The Complete Works of William Shakespeare, ed. David Bevington, 3rd ed. (Glenview, Ill.: Scott, Foresman, 1980), 870. References to Shakespeare's plays, with titles abridged, will be given from this edition. 1. Malin Åkerström, *Betrayal and Betrayers: The Sociology of Treachery* (New Brunswick, N.J.: Transaction, 1991). 2. John Banville, *The Untouchable* (New York: Knopf, 1997), 349; in Italian translation as *L'intoccabile* (Parma: Guanda, 1988), 356. 3. Judith N. Shklar, *Ordinary Vices* (Cambridge: Harvard University Press, Belknap Press, 1984), 140; in Italian translation as *Vizi comuni* (Bologna: Il Mulino, 1986), 167.

4. Joseph Conrad, *Under Western Eyes* (New York: Anchor Books/ Doubleday, 1963), 30; in Italian translation as *Con gli occhi dell'Occidente* (Milan: Garzanti, 1973), 68.

5. Ibid.

6. Georg Simmel, *Soziologie: Untersuchungen über die Formen der Vergesellschaft* (Leipzig: Dunker & Humblot, 1908); in Italian translation as *Sociologia* (Milan: Edizioni di Comunità, 1989), 501, 502; quoted from Simmel, *The Sociology of Georg Simmel,* trans., ed., and intro. Kurt H. Wolff (Glencoe, Ill.: Free Press, 1950), 379, 383–84.

7. Paul Auster, *Leviathan* (New York: Viking, 1992), 61; in Italian translation as *Il Leviatano* (Parma: Guanda, 1992), 64.

8. Shklar, *Ordinary Vices,* 142; *Vizi comuni,* 169.

9. Auster, *Leviathan,* 62, 61.

10. Henry Green, *Doting* (New York: Viking, 1952); in Italian translation by Stefania Bertola as *Passioni* (Turin: Einaudi, 1990).

11. Franco La Cecla, *Il malinteso: Antropologia dell'incontro* (Rome: Laterza, 1997), 14.

12. Vladimir Jankélévitch, *Le je-ne-sais-quoi et le presque-rien,* 3 vols. (Paris: Seuil, 1980), 105; in Italian translation as *Il non-so-che e il quasi niente* (Genoa: Marietti, 1987).

13. See Tony Tanner, *Adultery in the Novel: Contract and Transgression* (Baltimore: Johns Hopkins University Press, 1984), 41.

14. Shklar, *Ordinary Vices,* 161.

15. Simmel, *Sociology,* 394; *Sociologia,* 508.

16. Simmel, *Sociology,* 394; *Sociologia,* 509.

17. James Hillman, *Puer Papers,* ed. Hillman (Irving, Texas: Spring Publications, 1987); in Italian translation as *Puer Aeternus* (Milan: Adelphi, 1999). See Hillman, *Senex & Puer: An Aspect of the Historical and Psychological Present,* ed. Glen Slater (Putnam, Conn.: Spring Publications, 2005), 196–97.

18. Pierre Vidal-Naquet, "Flavius Josèphe, ou, Du bon usage de la trahison," preface to Flavius Josephus, *La guerre des juifs* (Paris: Editions de Minuit, 1977); in Italian translation as *Il buon uso del tradimento: Flavio Giuseppe e la guerra guidaica* (Rome: Editori Riuniti, 1992). Vidal-Naquet shows how Flavius Josephus, precisely by betraying his people when he sided with the Romans, guaranteed their salvation and well-being.

19. Karl Abraham et al., *Bugiardi e traditori* (Turin: Bollati Boringhieri, 1994).

20. Shklar, *Ordinary Vices*.

21. Robert Hogan and Joyce Hogan, "The Mask of Integrity," in *Citizen Espionage: Studies in Trust and Betrayal*, ed. Theodore R. Sarbin et al. (Westport, Conn.: Praeger, 1994), 93–105, esp. 95.

22. For these and other similar accounts, see Leigh Cato, *Her Version: True Stories of Love, Betrayal and Renewal—Women Talk about the Men They Have Shared as Husbands and Lovers* (New York: Penguin, 1995), 38; Cato, *She Said, She Said: Women's Stories of Love, Betrayal, and the Men They Have Shared as Husbands and Lovers* (Vancouver: Whitecap, 1996), 36.

23. Hillman, *Senex & Puer*, 211; *Puer Aeternus*, 46.

24. Banville, *The Untouchable*, 45, 131; *L'intoccabile*, 49, 136.

CHAPTER TWO

Epigraph. Robert Musil, "The Perfecting of a Love," trans. Eithne Wilkins and Ernst Kaiser, *Botteghe Oscure* 18 (Autumn 1956): 175, 225, esp. 205; in Italian translation as "Il compimento dell'amore," in Musil, *Incontri* (Turin: N.p., 1964), 38.

1. Hannah Arendt, *The Human Condition*, 2nd ed. (Chicago: University of Chicago Press, 1998), 244; in Italian translation as *La condizione umana* (Milan: Bompiani, 1994), 244.

2. Joseph Conrad, *Under Western Eyes* (New York: Anchor Books/ Doubleday, 1963).

3. Ibid., 30.

4. Arendt, *The Human Condition*, 190; *La condizione umana*, 190.

5. Ibid.

6. Arendt, *The Human Condition*, 237.

7. Hannah Arendt, *Vita Activa: Oder, Vom tätigen Leben* (Stuttgart: Kohlhammer, 1960); in Italian translation as *Vita activa* (Milan: Bompiani, 1994), 181.

8. Georg Simmel, *The Sociology of Georg Simmel*, trans., ed., and intro. Kurt H. Wolff (Glencoe, Ill.: Free Press, 1950), 310; *Sociologia* (Milan: Edizioni di Comunità, 1989), 294.

9. Simmel, *Sociology*, 315; *Sociologia*, 298.

10. Jacqueline Amati Mehler, Simona Argentieri, and Jorge Canestri, *La babele dell'inconscio: Lingue madre e lingue straniere nella dimensione psicoanalitica* (Milan: Cortina, 1990), 384–90; in English translation by Jill Whitelaw-Cucco as *The Babel of the Unconscious: Mother Tongue and*

Foreign Languages in the Psychoanalytical Dimension (Madison, Conn.: International Universities Press, 1993), 275–89.

11. John Banville, *The Untouchable* (New York: Knopf, 1997), 21, 33–34.

12. Franco La Cecla, *Il malinteso: Antropologia dell'incontro* (Rome: Laterza, 1997), 156.

13. Clara Sereni, *Il gioco dei Regni* (Florence: Giunti, 1993), 412.

14. Luigi Pirandello, *Uno, nessuno e centomila* (Milan: Feltrinelli, 1993); in English translation, with an introduction, by William Weaver as *One, No One, and One Hundred Thousand* (Boston: Endanos Press, 1990).

CHAPTER THREE

1. Dante, *The Divine Comedy*, vol. 1, *Inferno*, translated, with an introduction, notes, and commentary, by Mark Musa (Harmondsworth: Penguin, 1984), canto 34, lines 61–63, p. 381.

2. Mario Brelich, *L'opera del tradimento* (Milan: Adelphi, 1989); in English translation by Raymond Rosenthal as *The Work of Betrayal* (Marlboro, Vt.: Marlboro Press, 1988), 20–21.

3. Jorge Luis Borges, "Three Versions of Judas," in *Labyrinths: Selected Stories & Other Writings*, ed. Donald A. Yates and James E. Irby (New York: New Directions, 1962), 96; in Italian translation as "Tre versioni di Giuda," in *Finzioni* (Turin: Einaudi, 1997), 156.

4. Brelich, *Work of Betrayal*, 26–27, 29.

5. William Klassen, *Judas: Betrayer or Friend of Jesus?* (Minneapolis: Fortress Press, 1966); in Italian translation as *Giuda* (Milan: Bompiani, 1999).

6. Mario Brelich discusses this topic brilliantly in *L'opera del tradimento*.

7. See James Hillman, *Senex & Puer: An Aspect of the Historical and Psychological Present*, ed. Glen Slater (Putnam, Conn.: Spring Publications, 2005), 200–201; in Italian translation by Matelda Giuliani Talarico as *Senex et Puer: Tradimento* (Venice: Marsilio, 1973). See also Hillman, *Puer Papers*, ed. Hillman (Irving, Texas: Spring Publications, 1987); in Italian as *Puer Aeternus* (Milan: Adelphi, 1999).

8. Borges, *Labyrinths*, 98, 99; *Finzioni*, 159–60.

9. The text on which my remarks are based is Lytton Strachey, *Elizabeth and Essex: A Tragic History* (New York: Harcourt, Brace, 1928); in Italian translation as *Elisabetta e il Conte di Essex* (Milan: Tea, 1981).

10. By role betrayal I refer to the failure of an actor in society to sustain his or her social role when there are strong expectations that such a role be played coherently and competently. Unlike the "role distance" that, according to Erving Goffman, is a negation of the virtual self that does not necessarily interrupt either the "gaming encounter" or its "frame," role betrayal is a true and proper negation of both that role and that frame. In role betrayal all of the actors involved in the interaction—precisely because they are surprised to find their expectations disappointed—are suddenly left without a playbook, without a script. Role betrayal and abandonment on the part of one of the subjects becomes betrayal of a specific interaction. What is attacked is the interaction: the object of the betrayal is not one subject or another, but rather the interaction.

11. Strachey, *Elizabeth and Essex*, 170, 172.

12. Strachey, Elizabeth and Essex, 172; *Elisabetta e il Conte di Essex*, 203.

13. Erving Goffman, *Encounters: Two Studies in the Sociology of Interaction* (Indianapolis: Bobbs-Merrill, 1961), 55–56; in Italian translation as *Espressione e identità* (Milan: Mondadori, 1979), 53–54.

14. Strachey, *Elizabeth and Essex*, 176–77; *Elisabetta e il Conte di Essex*, 208.

15. Strachey, *Elizabeth and Essex*, 228; *Elisabetta e il Conte di Essex*, 268.

16. Strachey, *Elizabeth and Essex*, 237; *Elisabetta e il Conte di Essex*, 277–78.

CHAPTER FOUR

Epigraph. Quoted from Baldesar Castiglione, *The Book of the Courtier*, trans. and intro. George Bull, rev. ed. (London: Penguin, 1976), 138. Pietro Bembo is speaking.

1. Anthony Giddens, *The Transformation of Intimacy: Sexuality, Love and Eroticism in Modern Societies* (Cambridge: Polity Press, 1992), 154–55; in Italian translation as *La trasformazione dell'intimità* (Bologna: Il Mulino, 1992).

2. Javier Marías, *Corazón tan blanco*, in English translation by Margaret Jull Costa as *A Heart So White* (London: Harvill, 1995), 133–34; in Italian translation as *Un cuore così bianco* (Rome: Donzelli, 1992), 138.

3. Harold Pinter, *Betrayal*, in *Harold Pinter Plays: Four* (London: Eyre Methuen, 1981); in Italian translation as *Tradimenti* (Turin: Einaudi, 1978).

4. What Goffman calls "tactful inattention" is such forms of discretion as pretending not to see things or hear words that might be embarrassing. See Erving Goffman, *The Presentation of Self in Everyday Life* (Woodstock, N.Y.: Overlook Press, 1973), 230; in Italian translation by Margherita Ciacci as *La vita quotidiana come rappresentazione* (Bologna: Il Mulino, 1997).

5. Goffman, *Presentation of Self*, 112.

6. Georg Simmel, "Exkurs über den Adel," in his *Soziologie*; "The Secret and the Secret Society," in *The Sociology of Georg Simmel*, trans. Kurt H. Wolff (Glencoe, Ill.: Free Press, 1950), 305–76, esp. 322; "Il segreto e le società segrete," in *Sociologia* (Milan: Edizioni di Comunità, 1989), 302.

7. On the formation of the private sphere, see Richard Sennett, *The Fall of Public Man* (New York: Vintage, 1978); in Italian translation as *Il declino dell'uomo pubblico* (Milan: Bompiani, 1980). On the relevance that intimacy took on and on its transformation, see, among many studies, Giddens, *The Transformation of Intimacy* (*La trasformazione dell'intimità*), and Norbert Elias, *Über den Prozess der Zivilisation*, 2 vols. (Basel: Haus zum Falken, 1939), in English translation by Edmond Jephcott as *The Civilizing Process: Sociogenetic and Psychogenetic Investigations*, with some notes and corrections by the author, ed. Eric Dunning, Johan Goudsblom, and Stephen Mennet, rev. ed. (Oxford: Blackwell, 2000); in Italian translation as *Il processo di civilizzazione* (Bologna: Il Mulino, 1982–83).

8. Simmel, "The Secret," in *Sociology*, 322; "Il segreto," 308.

9. Simmel, "The Secret," 329; "Il segreto," 308.

10. Simmel, "The Secret," 315; "Il segreto," 298.

11. Marías, *Un cuore così bianco*, 138.

12. Simmel, "The Secret," 315; "Il segreto," 298.

13. Simmel, "The Secret," 315–16, 321; "Il segreto," 301.

14. Junichiro Tanizaki, *The Key*, trans. Howard Hibbett (New York: Knopf, 1961); in Italian translation by Satoko Taguchi as *La chiave* (Milan: Bompiani, 1964).

15. Tanizaki, *The Key*, 4; *La chiave*, 16.

16. Tanizaki, *The Key*, 11; *La chiave*, 20.

17. Tanizaki, *The Key*, 55; *La chiave*, 47.

18. Tanizaki, *The Key*, 58; *La chiave*, 48.

19. Remo Bodei, *Geometria delle passioni: Paura, speranza, felicità; Filosofia e uso politico* (Milan: Feltrinelli, 1991), 145.

20. Pinter, *Betrayal*, 172.

21. See Phyllis Greenacre, "La natura del tradimento e il carattere dei traditori," in *Bugiardi e traditori*, Karl Abraham et al. (Turin: Bollati Boringhieri, 1994), 106.

22. Pinter, *Betrayal*, 185.

23. Ibid., 166.

24. Frank S. Pittman, *Private Lies: Infidelity and the Betrayal of Intimacy* (New York: Norton, 1989); in Italian translation as *Bugie private* (Rome: Astrolabio, 1991).

25. Marías, *A Heart So White*, 136; *Un cuore così bianco*, 141.

26. Mme de La Fayette, *La princesse de Clèves*, in English translation by Michael G. Paulson and Tamara Alvarez-Detrell as *Madame de La Fayette's* The Princess of Clèves: *A New Translation* (Lanham, Md.: University Press of America, 1993), 99; in Italian translation as *La principessa di Clèves* (Milan: Garzanti, 1988), 98.

27. This fine and perspicacious definition can be found in Maria Ciambelli, Fiorangela Oneroso, and Gabriele Pulli, eds., *Il segreto e la psicoanalisi* (Naples: Gnocchi, 1996); see in particular Maria Teresa Messina, "Doppio segreto," in ibid., 232.

CHAPTER FIVE

1. Karl Marx, *The Communist Manifesto* (London: Penguin, 2002), 223.

2. See Franco Moretti, *Il romanzo di formazione* (Milan: Garzanti, 1986); in English translation as *The Way of the World: The* Bildungsroman *in European Culture*, trans. Albert Sbragia, new ed. (London: Verso, 2000).

3. Judith N. Shklar, *Ordinary Vices* (Cambridge: Harvard University Press, Belknap Press, 1984), 163; in Italian translation as *Vizi comuni* (Bologna: Il Mulino, 1986), 196.

4. Dante, *The Divine Comedy*, vol. 1, *Inferno*, canto 32, lines 13, 77–123, translated by Mark Musa (Harmondsworth: Penguin, 1984), 363, 364–66.

5. Niccolò Machiavelli, *Il Principe* (Florence: Club degli editori, 1972), 77, quoted from *The Prince*, trans. Harvey L. Mansfield Jr., 2nd ed. (Chicago: University of Chicago Press, 1998), 69, 70.

6. Machiavelli, *The Prince*, 70.

7. Baltasar Gracián y Morales, *Aqudeza y arte de ingenio* (Madrid: Editorial Castalia, 1969), in English translation by Christopher Maurer as *The Art of Worldly Wisdom: A Pocket Oracle* (New York: Doubleday, 1992); in Italian translation as *Oracolo manuale e arte di prudenza* (Parma: Guanda, 1986).

8. Torquato Accetto, *Della dissimulazione onesta* (1641), ed. Salvatore S. Nigro (Turin: Einaudi, 1997), 59–60.

9. Salvatore Nigro, in ibid., xviii–xix.

10. Ibid., xxii.

11. Shklar, *Ordinary Vices*, 140; *Vizi comuni*, 167.

12. Quoted in Shklar, *Ordinary Vices*, 178; *Vizi comuni*, 210.

13. Shklar, *Ordinary Vices*, 191; *Vizi comuni*, 224.

14. Allan Silver, "'Trust' in Social and Political Theory," in *The Challenge of Social Control: Citizenship and Institution Building in Modern Society; Essays in Honor of Morris Janowitz*, ed. Gerald D. Suttles and Mayer N. Zald (Norwood, N.J.: Ablex, 1985), 52–67, esp. 55.

15. Georg Simmel, "The Secret," in *The Sociology of Georg Simmel*, trans. Kurt H. Wolff (Glencoe, Ill.: Free Press, 1950), 308; "Il segreto," in *Sociologia* (Milan: Edizioni di Comunità, 1989), 298.

16. Niklas Luhmann, *Trust and Power: Two Works* (New York: John Wiley, 1988); originally published as *Vertrauen* and *Macht*.

17. Peter Beinert, "The Odd Logic of a Spy's Defenders," *New York Times*, January 19, 1999.

18. Simmel, "The Secret," in *Sociology*, 326; "Il segreto," in *Sociologia*, 308.

19. Italo Calvino, "Solidarietà," in his *Prima che tu dica pronto* (Milan: Mondadori, 1993), quoted from the English translation by Tim Parks as "Solidarity," in Calvino, *Numbers in the Dark and Other Stories* (New York: Pantheon Books, 1995), 20–22.

20. Richard Sennett, *Corrosion of Character: The Personal Consequences of Work in the New Capitalism* (New York: Norton, 1998), 25; in Italian translation by Mirko Tavosanis as *L'uomo flessibile: Le conseguenze del nuovo capitalismo sulla vita personale* (Milan: Feltrinelli, 1999), 23.

21. Sennett, *Corrosion of Character*, 24; *L'uomo flessibile*, 22.

22. See Sherry Turkle, *Life on the Screen: Identity in the Age of the Internet* (New York: Simon & Schuster, 1995); in Italian translation as *La vita sullo schermo* (Milan: Apogeo, 1997).

23. Turkle, *Life on the Screen*, 13.

24. Amy Harmon, "On-line Trail to an Off-line Killing," *New York Times*, April 30, 1998, with a follow-up article August 5, 1998; Pamela Licalzi O'Connell, "Screen Grab: Many Sites to Confess One's Sins," *New York Times*, September 3, 1998.

25. "Computers; Private Eyes," *New York Times Magazine*, May 24, 1998.

26. On this point, see Anthony Giddens, *The Consequences of Modernity* (Stanford: Stanford University Press, 1990); in Italian translation as *Le consequenze della modernità* (Bologna: Il Mulino, 1994).

Index

Accetto, Torquato, 107
action, social, 38, 40
adolescence, 24–25, 78–79
adultery, 2, 8, 94; Hawthorne and, 122
affiliations, 3, 10, 75, 103, 120–21; and
the Internet, 123, 125, 126; Judas
and, 56; multiple, 104, 111, 113, 114,
115, 125, 126. *See also* membership
Alexander VI, pope, 106
alterity, 17, 44, 79. *See also* other, the
ambiguity, 1, 3, 5, 45, 57
ambivalence, 4, 42, 45, 79, 103; in
Hamlet, 97; in Judas and Peter, 49
America Online, 126
Arendt, Hannah, 36–37, 38, 40
Auster, Paul (*Leviathan*), 14, 15
autonomy, 79, 88, 107

Balzac, Honoré de, 104
Banville, John (*The Untouchable*), 10,
34–35, 43
bed, bedroom, 76, 81
Beinert, Peter, 115
being for oneself, being for the other,
45–48

betrayal: as act, 4, 8, 44; adolescents
and, 24, 78–79; archetypes of, 49–
50, 56–57; as asymmetrical, 22; as
asynchronic, 22–24; as banal, 120,
121; and change, 21; complicity
in, 44; concealment and, 82–83;
culture of, 115; and death, 41–42;
definition of, 1, 6, 7–8, 24, 121;
emotions and, 25–31, 127–28; fascination of, 31–35; forms of, 1, 8,
108; frequency of, 2, 3, 104, 120,
121; as a game, 34; and interaction,
3, 28, 122; and the Internet, 123–30;
of intimacy, 81; in literature, 2;
misunderstanding and, 44; moral
judgment of, 1, 2, 6, 31–32, 103, 105,
121; motivations for, 12, 31–32, 43,
46, 57, 74–77; as "ordinary vice,"
2, 27, 122; as pathological, 26, 27;
perceptions of, 17–20, 22–24, 84,
120; political, 2, 5, 104–6, 108,
111; private, 109–10; professional,
119–20; public, 104, 108, 109; as relational, 8, 28, 44–45; as a resource,
103–8;

Shakespeare, William, 2, 19, 32, 104;
  Coriolanus, 39–40, 47–48; *Hamlet*,
  97–102; *Henry the Fourth, Part II*,
  7; *King Lear*, 18–19, 103, 110, 111;
  Macbeth, 104; *Othello*, 18, 19, 49;
  Richard III, 26, 32–33, 104
Shklar, Judith N., 2, 14, 27, 105, 108–9
Silver, Allan, 110
Simmel, Georg, 45, 83; on discretion,
  79; on faithfulness and unfaithfulness, 13, 21; on knowing the
  self and others, 42, 112; on private
  property, 81; on relationships, 85
sin, 5, 103, 105
sincerity, 95, 96, 99, 107
socialization, 25, 26
social sciences, 27
society, 80, 103, 104, 111; complexity
  in, 111, 113
sociology, 3, 5–6, 12, 13, 27
solidarity, 118
spies, 32, 33–34, 114
subjectivity, 107, 108

Tanizaki, Junichiro (*The Key*), 86–88
Tanner, Tony, 2
time, 22–24, 30–31
Tirso de Molina (Gabriel Téllez), 107
Tolstoy, Leo, 2
trädere, 7–8, 51, 53, 78, 125
traitor, 10, 12, 27, 105, 118, 119; Calvino
  protagonist as, 116
transparency, 4, 42–43, 92, 93–94, 95

treachery, 26, 104, 105–6
treason, 5, 8, 108–9; Elizabeth and
  Essex and, 65, 66, 67, 68–70
Tripp, Linda, 122
trompe l'oeil, 107
trust, 82–83, 110–11, 112, 113, 118–19; expectations of, 121; and interaction
  and intersubjectivity, 11, 29, 40, 41,
  42; in Internet groups, 124, 129; in
  Machiavelli, 106; need for, 1, 9, 41;
  primal, 25
Turkle, Sherry, 124
Tyrone, Shane O'Neill, 2nd earl of,
  62

United States Constitution, 108–9
United States Navy, 126
unpredictability, 36–37, 42
Updike, John, 2

values, 6, 105, 110, 119, 127
Versailles, court of, 81

We, 24, 29, 73, 119; abandonment of
  the, 9, 21, 78; in Calvino, 117; definition of the, 3, 9–10; Elizabeth
  and Essex as a, 59, 62, 63–64, 65,
  67, 68, 69, 71; forms of, 12–13; and
  the Internet, 123; Judas and, 49, 51;
  multiple, 115–16, 119–21; Peter and,
  49, 57, 58; ways to betray the, 12–13
Web. *See* Internet, the
Willey, Kathleen, 122